DATE DUE

DEC. 01.1998			
GAYLORD			PRINTED IN U.S.A.

THE SERVICE FOCUS

DEVELOPING WINNING GAME PLANS FOR SERVICE COMPANIES

THE SERVICE FOCUS

DEVELOPING WINNING GAME PLANS FOR SERVICE COMPANIES

John C. Shaw, C.P.A.
Senior Partner
Touche Ross & Co.

Dow Jones-Irwin
Homewood, Illinois 60430

© RICHARD D. IRWIN, INC., 1990

Dow Jones-Irwin is a trademark of Dow Jones & Company, Inc.

This publication is designed to provide accurate
and authoritative information in regard to the subject matter
covered. It is sold with the understanding that the
publisher is not engaged in rendering legal, accounting, or
other professional service. If legal advice or other expert
assistance is required, the services of a competent
professional person should be sought.

*From a Declaration of Principles jointly adopted by a Committee
of the American Bar Association and a Committee of Publishers.*

Sponsoring editor: Jim Childs
Project editor: Paula M. Buschman
Production manager: Diane Palmer
Jacket design: Mike Finkelman
Compositor: Weimer Typesetting Co., Inc.
Typeface: 11/13 Century Schoolbook
Printer: Arcata Graphics/Kingsport

Library of Congress Cataloging-in-Publication Data

Shaw, John C. (John Clark), 1933–
    The service focus: developing winning game plans for service
        companies/ by John C. Shaw.
            p.   cm.
    Includes index.
    ISBN 1-55623-239-X
    1. Service industries—United States—Management.   2. Strategic
    planning—United States.   I. Title.
    HD9981.5.S53   1990
    658.4'012—dc20   89–35045
                                                                    CIP

Printed in the United States of America

2 3 4 5 6 7 8 9 0 K 6 5 4 3 2 1 0

This book is dedicated to
James Foster Hansley, Jr.
December 6, 1957–November 26, 1988

He set the standard for us all

FOREWORD

As we move into the last decade of the 20th century, a century which witnessed a transition from an agrarian to a service economy with barely a pause for an industrial economy, the question of how we lead our enterprises and our nation is on the mind of every thoughtful manager. The old management tools, tools designed during the first 75 years of this century, don't work any more. Worse, those old tools are harmful and counter-productive to service organizations. The dilemma we face, of course, is straightforward—if the "old medicine" doesn't work any more, what "new medicine" do we take instead.

The question of what new medicine we take in place of the former prescription is critical to our country's economic survival in the "global village" in which we live. The global realities with which we must live—including an economically united Europe; the industrialization of the Pacific Rim; Japan's transition to a service economy; not to mention the entrepreneurial spirit which has been unleashed in the Communist World—*demand* that we "get our act together" and compete from a position of strength. The "old medicine"—a prescription from the past—does not work in the world of new realities.

My partner, Jack Shaw, has devoted nearly his entire career with Touche Ross consulting to service companies, government, and not-for-profit organizations, on the subject of service-sector management. Based on his consulting work with literally hundreds of our firm's service-sector clients, Jack has developed the concepts and the tools which may replace the old medicine with a new prescription which works.

The concepts and tools which Jack puts forth in this, his latest book, are more than theoretical, ivory tower ideas which *may* work in practice. The fact is that the concepts and tools are integrated into an implementation process which is proven and *does* work in practice. Jack and our firm's clients have worked hand in hand for years developing and refining the approaches to service-sector management which are recommended in this book.

Chapter 1 of Jack's work outlines the old medicine, the prescriptions which *may* have worked in the past for the industrial-sector, and documents why such concepts are not effective, or at best, different in their outcomes for the service sector. Chapter 2 details the new prescription in the form of the tools and concepts which work for service enterprises. The remainder of the book is devoted to the process of implementation, because no matter how insightful or creative the new prescription, strategic thinking which is not implemented is worse than no strategy at all.

Let's hope that Jack's work will influence service-sector managers, and hopefully, our country toward the development of "winning game plans" for the future.

Edward A. Kangas, C.P.A.
Managing Partner and
Chief Executive Officer
Touche Ross & Co.

PREFACE

SERVICE COMPANY MANAGEMENT IS DIFFERENT

Not withstanding the well-known facts concerning the impact and the importance of service-sector enterprises on the American economy, it is interesting that among America's most admired corporations, the top 10 include only one service firm—Wal-Mart Stores. Furthermore, in the "*88 Gallop Survey*," Consumer's Perceptions Concerning the Quality of American Products and Services, Sears, Roebuck, & Co. with 13 percent, was the only service company among the five companies most frequently associated with high quality. The magazine *Business Month*, nominated only one service company—Wal-Mart—in their survey of the five best-managed companies. The magazine's Honorable Mention category, however, included 8 service companies out of the 15 receiving mention. Finally, the prestigious Malcolm Baldridge Award for quality did not name a service organization in a category reserved for services.

Why are service companies so frequently omitted from the ranks of excellent organizations? When comparisons between service enterprises and industrial organizations are made, why is it that service companies seem to suffer by comparison? Is there some fundamental reason why service companies and industrial companies can't be compared logically? We assume that the differences between service companies and industrial enterprises are much greater than similarities, and that comparisons are impossible to make. Therefore, the principles of management as well as strategic concepts and tools that were developed over the past 50–75 years for industrial organizations are inappropriate for service organizations. This book not only elaborates on the differences between the sectors but also offers a set of concepts, tools, and processes that are appropriate to the strategic management of service enterprises.

This book walks the tightrope between theory and practice—perhaps an impossible mission. On the theory side, we have tested our concepts with the professors and the students at both the Stanford University Graduate School of Business, where I taught in 1982 and 1983, and at The Wharton School of the University of Pennsylvania, where I currently teach as a visiting professor. The professors, students, and administrators of both institutions have been extremely helpful and supportive. On the practice side, the concepts, tools and processes have been successfully implemented during scores of consulting assignments. In addition, on the practice side, I have received support from the men and women who have attended service management courses offered in the executive education program at the Aresty Institute of The Wharton School.

Finally, as we integrated theory with practice, we analyzed the financial *and* economic performance of over 300 companies of *The Fortune Service 500*. The appendix to this book describes the methodology used to correlate both financial and economic performance of the 300 companies. Chapter 8 highlights our assessment of the underlying themes pursued by both organizations that achieved a sustained competitive advantage and organizations that did not. We believe that the quantitative analyses support the concepts in this work.

This book is a compilation of experience I have gained from clients and colleagues during a lifetime of work with industrial, service, government, and not-for-profit organizations. It is impossible to acknowledge all contributions individually, however, there are a few contributions too valuable to omit:

My wife, Nancy Shaw, has made a big difference both professionally and with her personal support.

All of my clients have helped enormously—particularly: Edward A. Brennan, Chairman and CEO, Sears, Roebuck and Co; Douglas E. Ebert, Sector Executive Vice President, Investment Banking, Manufacturers Hanover Corporation; William E. Flaherty, President and CEO, Blue Cross and Blue Shield of Florida; Richard A. Liddy, Chairman and COO, General American Insurance; Earl H. Orser, Chairman and CEO, London Life Insurance Company; Leonard D. Schaeffer, President and CEO, Blue Cross of California; John W. Teets, Chairman and CEO, The Greyhound Corporation; E. Dean Werries, Chairman, President, and CEO, The Fleming Companies; and Robert C. Winters, Chairman and CEO, The Prudential.

My colleagues at Stanford and Wharton also put the seal of creditability on my efforts, including; Professor Gerald R. Faulhaber, with whom I teach at The Wharton School; Charles Hallaway, Associate Dean, The Stanford Graduate School of Business; Professor David Jamison, The Stanford Graduate School of Business; Russell E. Palmer, Dean of The Wharton School, and Professor Paul Tiffany of The Wharton School.

My Touche Ross colleagues all have been extremely supportive, particularly: William Atkins, Charles L. Biggs, Donald A. Curtis, Thomas L. Doorley, John Harrison, Don C. Hawley, Edward A. Kangas, Pat A. Loconto, Christopher M. Neenan, William T. Potvin, J. Thomas Presby, James E. Seitz, and Philip E. Strause.

April, 1989, New York   **John C. Shaw**

CONTENTS

PART I

THE CONCEPTS

OVERVIEW OF THE SECTION

We introduced this text as a book that deals with processes that work. Part I begins the trip through the various processes by introducing a basic set of tools that are employed throughout the text as a consistent framework for analysis. The tools and techniques involved, with the exception of the client/customer service spectrum, have been introduced by other writers, teachers, and strategy consultants; however, we use both the new and "used" tools in a unique manner. The employment of tools recommended in this section is unique because they are introduced as a set. The value of the concepts employed rests in their combined application.

The following tools are described in greater depth in Chapters 1 and 2:

The service life cycle.
Client/customer service spectrum.
The creation of service value.
The service-value chain.

A thorough understanding of the framework for analysis suggested in Part I is a prerequisite for full use of the process or flow of strategic management activities, which comprise the remainder of the book. See pages 2–4 for an overview of strategic management processes that are described in Parts II-IV.

PART II
"Where Are We?" versus Competition (The Strategic-Assessment
Process)

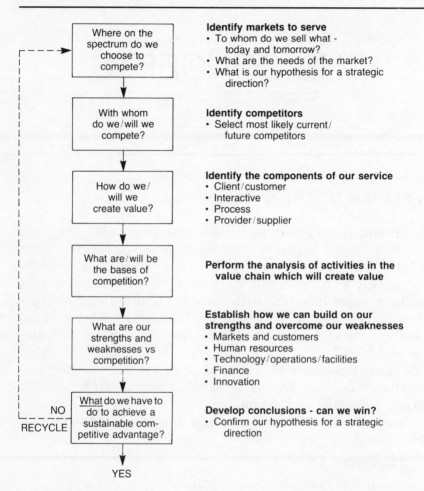

Where on the spectrum do we choose to compete?	**Identify markets to serve** • To whom do we sell what - today and tomorrow? • What are the needs of the market? • What is our hypothesis for a strategic direction?
With whom do we/will we compete?	**Identify competitors** • Select most likely current/ future competitors
How do we/ will we create value?	**Identify the components of our service** • Client/customer • Interactive • Process • Provider/supplier
What are/will be the bases of competition?	**Perform the analysis of activities in the value chain which will create value**
What are our strengths and weaknesses vs competition?	**Establish how we can build on our strengths and overcome our weaknesses** • Markets and customers • Human resources • Technology/operations/facilities • Finance • Innovation
What do we have to do to achieve a sustainable competitive advantage?	**Develop conclusions - can we win?** • Confirm our hypothesis for a strategic direction

NO
RECYCLE

YES

Following Chapters 1 and 2, this section concludes with
Chapter 3—Missing: A Strategic Direction. The materials introduced in this chapter are intended to help the reader pos-
tulate or establish a hypothesis as to "what the business might
be" before launching into a series of chapters that may be used
as a process for confirming or rejecting this hypothesis. Chapter 3 also introduces the concept of planning units (or business

PART III
"Where Are We Going?" (The Strategic-Direction Process)

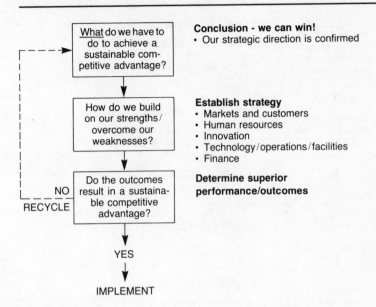

What do we have to do to achieve a sustainable competitive advantage?

Conclusion - we can win!
• Our strategic direction is confirmed

How do we build on our strengths / overcome our weaknesses?

Establish strategy
• Markets and customers
• Human resources
• Innovation
• Technology / operations / facilities
• Finance

NO
RECYCLE

Do the outcomes result in a sustainable competitive advantage?

Determine superior performance/outcomes

YES

IMPLEMENT

units), which provide a market-driven focus for the sections on process that follow.

PART IV
"How Do We Get There?" (Translating Strategy into Action)

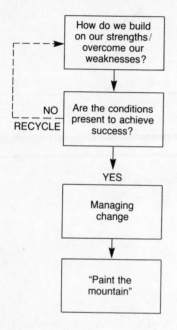

Develop action plans

- Markets and customers
- Human resources
- Technology/operations/facilities
- Finance
- Innovation

Diagnose our readiness for change

- The five conditions which must be present in order to translate strategy into action

Implement

- Action plans and results

Success

- Our visions sustain us

CHAPTER 1

THE BIG DIFFERENCE: SERVICE VERSUS MANUFACTURING COMPANIES

Service companies are in the throes of a turbulent transition. Deregulation, globalization, more powerful foreign competitors, and the growing volatility of markets make it harder than ever for service institutions to compete effectively. Service companies must sharpen their competitive edge, as America's prosperity increasingly depends on their superior performance. The service sector accounts for more than two-thirds of America's gross national product, for about 75 percent of the work force, and for up to 90 percent of new employment.

Yet, many service companies stagger under the pressure of this new, competitive environment. At the core of this problem is an approach to planning and strategy that continues to embrace lessons learned from older manufacturing origins. In the absence of any service-specific tools, service managers are inappropriately applying the lessons and models derived from the industrial sector to their service companies. This dangerous tendency is too often endorsed by business scholars and management consultants, who tend to view service companies in the context of their manufacturing experience. The tendency is further reinforced by securities analysts and business journalists, whose analyses of service corporations are governed largely by manufacturing criteria. Even the most serious writers on planning and strategy imply that what works for the smaller manufacturing sector of the economy will work for the much larger service sector. As services assume greater roles in

America's domestic economy and foreign trade, the misguided approaches to planning and strategy will have increasingly adverse consequences.

One need not look far to find examples of service companies that have blundered or failed by misapplying the planning and strategic tools used by industrial enterprises:

• People's Express succeeded almost overnight by focusing on a specific segment of the air travel market. It offered low fares, no frills, and a truly dedicated cadre of employees, whose service was characterized by enthusiasm, loyalty, and informality. Having grown restless with what it perceived as limited success and failing to recognize the ingredients of its success, the airline—like many manufacturing companies—went for growth and market share. Anticipating service to multiple markets, People's Express added capacity and acquired other companies. Higher fixed costs forced it to chase demand. The company finally lost its customer focus, and service suffered. Passengers became so disgruntled that they dubbed the airline "People's Distress." The airline faced bankruptcy in 1987 and was absorbed by Texas Air Corporation.

• Some money center and large regional banks' poor performance resulted largely from their neglect to recognize that unlike industrial concerns, banking is a service rather than a product business. Eager to take advantage of deregulation and the worldwide growth of financial services, they expanded around the globe, seldom tailoring their organizations or services to the different markets they sought to serve. The banks sometimes treated international markets as if they were extensions of local domestic markets with which they were most familiar. The behavior of many bank managers suggested that they thought there was something so distinct about their "products" that they could achieve growth and expand share by approaching divergent markets in similar ways. The banks' obsession with growth and share was abundantly endorsed by securities analysts and institutional investors.

• Airlines and banking are not the only service industries that have suffered from emulating manufacturing models. In their quest for growth and economies of scale, many life insurance companies have invested heavily in infrastructure—adding enormous fixed costs. The quest has continued despite the fact that, as Robert C. Winters, chairman of The Prudential, has said, "No one has demonstrated that there are economies of scale in the life insurance industry." The need to absorb fixed costs has forced the companies to push existing "products" long after many of the "products" became obsolete. Ignoring the highly personal service nature of their business, health maintenance organizations (HMOs) expanded from their limited but secure geographical markets into other states. The generous availability of capital from enthusiastic bankers also encouraged the HMOs to expand their services into such peripheral areas as homes for senior citizens. Damaged by their manufacturing-like quest for growth, size, and economies of scale, HMOs are now in one of the worst shakeouts ever in the health care business. The number of HMO plans has grown twice as fast as enrollment in the plans, and premiums cannot often cover rising patient care and operating costs.

THE SERVICE SECTOR'S SEARCH FOR IDENTITY

Despite the prominent role that services now play in the U.S. economy, service managers seek not only to look more like manufacturers but to sound more like them. Clear evidence of this is the widespread tendency among service managers to refer to their services as products. In a recent press interview about his corporate strategy, for example, the chairman of a financial service conglomerate said, "The life insurance (we) sell is a great way to create a relationship with a household. If that turns out to be an efficient distribution system for other products, so be it." In a public discussion about his approach to service late last year, the CEO of another financial service corporation said, "In a commodity-like business like ours, service is the only way to create product differentiation." These senior executives have a lot of company among commercial and investment bankers and brokers who talk about capital market products, corporate finance products, and investment products.

Just as service managers aspire to look and sound more like industrial managers, manufacturers are moving away from the traditional focus on product and adopting service concepts to improve performance. Business authors, writing about manufacturing companies, have added service to price and quality as an essential competitive weapon. They regularly cite success stories of industrial companies that have become more service-oriented. Corporate managers have buttressed this notion by touting the importance of customer orientation and service in manufacturing. In 1987, the Gallup Organization polled senior executives at 615 companies to gauge the relative importance of various factors in their competitiveness. The poll revealed that even manufacturing executives identified better service as important as higher quality.

The frequently unconscious wish among service-sector managers to look and sound like their peers in manufacturing stems from two factors. One of these factors is the premium that the American management "system" places on what is measurable and predictable. Accounting and financial processes tend to treat what is measurable and predictable as far more real than the processes, which are more difficult to measure. Since tangible products are more readily measured and controlled than intangible services, products command greater attention. The second factor is a lingering sense among purveyors of service that they are second-class citizens. One writer has traced this sense to an American loathing for the servitude implied by service.

The lowly status where services have been relegated is deeply rooted in economic history, which has been anything but kind to the service sector. As far back as the 18th century, Adam Smith, the father of classical economics, criticized the service sector's role in the economy. He wrote that services are "unproductive of any value because they do not fix or realize themselves in any permanent subject or vendible commodity which endures after labor is passed." A service, he said, "perishes in the very instant of its production." Economists in the early decades of this century defined the service component of the economy as a *residual,* that is, as the difference between total wages and the wages expended in the production of goods. They called this residual *unproductive labor.* Labor economists later defined nongoods wages as *immaterial goods.* Even in today's more tolerant environment, services are usually defined as *intangible products,* suggesting that they are somehow derived from manufacturing.

DEFINING SERVICES

Defining service in these terms reinforces the tendency among service companies to emulate industrial planning and strategic models. It is more accurate and effective to think of a service as something that changes the condition or status of its consumer in a fundamental way. Medical services, for example, affect the physical well-being of the patient; legal counseling affects the potential liability of a client; a hotel chain affects a traveler's comfort; an insurance policy affects the policyholder's risk profile. Because a service is consumed at the moment of production, who delivers the service—whether an investment banker or a telephone repairer—exerts a greater influence on quality than even the most sophisticated quality control system.

Since human needs, expectations, values, conditions, and status are subject to routine change, services are variable, unpredictable, and not susceptible to systemic control. By the same token, services must respond to a potentially infinite set of consumer conditions. Few executives have described services better than Leon Gorman, president of L. L. Bean, the Freeport, Maine mail-order house that leads its industry in quality of service. "A lot of people have fancy things to say about . . . service, including me," Gorman says, "but it's just a day-in, day-out, ongoing, never-ending, unremitting, persevering, compassionate type of activity." This view is echoed by Charles Sanford, chairman of Bankers Trust, one of the best performing banks in the United States. "People visit us from all over the world to understand the 'secret' of our success," Sanford says. "But there is no secret. It's just the day-to-day practice of the fundamentals, the blocking and tackling of our business."

As these characterizations of service suggest, the differences between goods-producing industrial enterprises and service enterprises are so pronounced that there is no empirical basis for comparison. But the tendency among service managers to define themselves in manufacturing terms is so great, the industrial bias in American business is so overwhelming, that comparing product with service and manufacturing with service enterprises is inevitable.

MANUFACTURING VERSUS SERVICE

The chart on the following page summarizes the fundamental differences between product and service firms with respect to various aspects of corporate planning and strategy. The first eight criteria relate to the generic differences between product and service. The last two criteria relate to broader competitive factors.

A cursory look at the chart shows why it is inappropriate to adapt manufacturing planning and strategic concepts to service institutions. The danger of transferring strategic concepts from one sector to the other becomes clearer when looking closely at the differences between manufacturing and service companies.

Standardization

As practiced by industrial companies, standardization entails disassembling or breaking a product into its components and constructing an assembly or other process to manufacture the product as efficiently as possible. Coupled with various means of managing manufacturing cost and quality, standardization allows industrial companies to achieve a greater focus on the product, product quality, and cost.

Any attempt to standardize a service shifts the focus away from the customer. Neglecting variability and flexibility in fa-

| | Impact on | |
Concept–Strategy	Product Firms	Service Firms
Standardization	Provides focus	Misplaces focus from the customer
Costing and pricing	Based on physical product	Based on perceptions of value
Productivity	Can be measured	Cannot be measured
Matching supply and demand	Managed through inventory	Managed largely through changes in behavior
Economies of scale	Permit unit costs to decline permanently	Permit unit costs to decline temporarily
Experience curve	Reduces unit costs through cumulative production	Improves quality and value
Growth/Size/Share	Directly influence profitability	Indirectly influence image
Risk of launching new product/service	Lower as a result of market testing	Higher as a result of greater reliance on customer trust
Barriers to entry	Based on product and/or technology focus	Based on human capital, customer base, and/or network
Implementation of change	Requires relatively few people	Requires widespread consensus and commitment

vor of standardization in service companies makes it impossible to change the condition of the customer and to satisfy the customer's needs. Moreover, the means of managing cost and quality, which accompany standardization in manufacturing, tend to add cost to a service without necessarily improving quality or productivity. It is true, of course, that some institutions offering more "commodity-like" services such as McDonald's, Burger King, H&R Block, and Hyatt Legal Services, for example, must have carefully managed processes to ensure both quality and productivity. But even those processes are competitively effective only when they focus on the customer rather than on the "service product."

Despite the ineffectiveness of product standardization to service companies, business scholars have encouraged the tendency. In his production-line approach to service, former Harvard Business School professor Theodore Levitt, says, "(Service firms) must think of themselves as performing manufacturing functions when it comes to their so-called 'service' activities. Only then will they begin to make some significant progress in improving the quality and efficiency of service in the modern economy."[1]

Costing and Pricing

In manufacturing companies, standard cost accounting techniques are applied to each step of the production process, including labor, materials, and various types of overhead, to arrive at a total product cost. A profit margin is then applied based on several considerations, including competition, and a price is established. This approach, often called "cost-based pricing," works because the cost of manufacturing and selling a tangible product can be measured physically.

By contrast, few services can be subjected to the precise control required for an effective standard cost system. Even if it were possible to determine the real cost of providing a service, it would be largely irrelevant in setting a price. To a greater extent than a product, the value of a service is based on the consumer's subjective perception of value. It is based on the effectiveness with which the consumer of the service perceives needs or expectations will be met by the service. The value of a service, as perceived by the consumer, hinges on the interaction between price and quality.

If anything, a "price-based costing" principle works far better in the services. Once the service is priced at a fair market value, the service provider must figure out how to produce the service at a cost that the price will cover and still allow enough room for a profit. Price-based costing is eloquently

[1]Theodore Levitt, "Production-Line Approach to Service," *Harvard Business Review,* September-October 1972, pp. 41–52. Copyright © 1972 by the President and Fellows of Harvard College. All rights reserved.

summarized by Stanley Marcus, the Chairman Emeritus of Neiman Marcus. "If the market is not willing to pay for what one has to offer," Marcus says, "then one has to ask, 'what can I remove and still maintain a reasonable quality of service that differentiates us from the masses?' It isn't easy."

Even though "cost-based pricing" is not suitable for the services, many industrial cost accountants and business scholars have promoted the notion that service can be treated like a product—or "industrialized"—and subjected to standard cost accounting techniques. Even such eminent scholars as Professor John Dearden of the Harvard Business School promotes this inappropriate manufacturing concept when he writes, "The very survival of some service companies depends on management's knowing the cost of its products."[2] By endorsing this notion, Dearden and others encourage service companies to collect and analyze cost data, which is expensive, time-consuming, and ultimately futile.

Productivity

Measuring productivity and, by extension, managing it based on specific output measures, is another manufacturing tool consistently misapplied to service companies. Productivity measures in manufacturing are straightforward. Output, the number of units, is divided by input, the sum of the factors required to produce the units. Commonly used measures are the ratio of output to hours worked, which is called labor productivity, and output per unit of capital input, a yardstick for capital productivity.

In services, however, there is no physically measurable output. Economists, therefore, substitute other inputs—often labor costs—over some measure of inflation. Using this ratio, they conclude that if labor costs grow slower than inflation, for example, productivity must be rising. This is wrong. Labor costs and other surrogates for service output do not work, and

---

[2]John Dearden, "Cost Accounting Comes to Service Industries," *Harvard Business Review*, September-October 1978, pp. 132–140. Copyright © 1978 by the President and Fellows of Harvard College. All rights reserved.

industrial productivity measures are misleading when applied to service companies. Academics, government statisticians, and management consultants, however, devote too much effort designing, refining, and applying these measures.

Productivity in the service sector deals with how a service organization can increase its effectiveness and efficiency in serving customers. Low cost, superior quality, and a strong service focus all ensure high productivity, which is reflected in consistently high or rising operating margins. Of course, there are several effective ways of measuring and monitoring productivity in some services, including sales per employee or value added per employee, which is the difference between the dollar value of sales or revenues and the dollar value of the goods and services purchased to generate those revenues.

Matching Supply and Demand

Another misguided effort to apply industrial concepts to service institutions relates to matching supply and demand. Like other manufacturing experience misapplications to the service sector, this one has prominent support from business academics. In an article entitled "Matching Supply and Demand in Service Industries," Harvard Business School professor Earl Sasser argues that in balancing supply and demand, service companies can learn a great deal from industrial companies.[3] In manufacturing, supply and demand are managed through inventory. Product-oriented organizations keep inventory at the factory where it is produced; at a distribution facility; or at a location close to or on the premises of the final consumer. Inventory is managed by minimizing its level consistent with high levels of customer service. Just-in-time (JIT) is an example of inventory management strategy. But neither JIT nor any other strategy available to manufacturers for matching supply and demand to achieve better customer service and lower inventory carrying costs is appropriate to the services. Why?

---

[3]W. Earl Sasser, "Matching Supply and Demand in Service Industries," *Harvard Business Review*, November-December 1976, pp. 133–140. Copyright © 1976 by the President and Fellows of Harvard College. All rights reserved.

Services are consumed at the moment of production and because the changing condition or status of a customer cannot be
stored.

The service equivalent of the manufacturers' cost of carrying inventory is the cost of idle capacity. In service companies, idle capacity consists of items such as empty hospital
beds, vacant hotel rooms, empty airline seats, and excess staff-
ing. Requiring a different set of management tools, idle capacity is managed by: hiring more part-time workers when strong
demand warrants it; closing excess capacity; or discounting
prices. Idle capacity in manufacturing can be used up by producing more goods and storing them for future consumption or
by reducing the work force. However, in the capital-intensive
service industries—airlines, health care, utilities, and telecommunications, for example—idle capacity is managed by reducing prices and offering incentives for filling it. Managing idle
capacity in the labor-intensive service industries such as public
accounting, personal care, and fast food requires sensitive, peo-
ple-oriented solutions that hinge on changes in the behavior of
both the customer and the service firm.

Economies of Scale

Economies of scale benefit industrial companies in the long
run by reducing the average unit cost of a product as the fixed
component of product costs is spread over greater output. Con-
trary to widespread belief, economies of scale do not benefit
service corporations in the same way. The reason has to do
with different cost structures between manufacturing and
service firms. Fixed costs in manufacturing constitute only between 15 and 30 percent of total costs. The remaining 70–85
percent of costs is attributed to the product and varies with the
volume of production during a given period. In fact, the variable costs disappear when the product is eliminated. In manufacturing, the fixed-cost component can be spread over
increasing volumes, affecting total product costs but not total
fixed costs even over a long period. The resulting improvement
in unit costs either can be passed to the customer as lower
prices that fuel further growth or be kept by the firm through

higher margins. Economies of scale in manufacturing, therefore, allow profitability to vary directly with volume and organization size. A higher volume of output is usually equated with greater profitability.

In service companies, on the other hand, fixed costs account for as much as 70–85 percent of total costs. In most service companies, few costs can be attributed to a specific service and, in many instances, only 15–30 percent is directly attributed to the organizational unit that produces the service. This substantial fixed-cost component encourages service companies to "chase" demand to absorb the fixed costs through increased volume. But, in contrast to manufacturers, the potentially lower costs are reflected neither in lower prices nor improved margins. Prices are not reduced because it is generally impossible to determine which specific services are affected and which services fuel profitable growth. Meanwhile, margins remain stable or decline because capacity is often added in large increments which, on average, boosts fixed costs faster than volume. Unit costs may, therefore, decline temporarily as capacity becomes fully utilized, but they will again rise as additional capacity is brought on line to serve real or potential increases in demand. Exhibit 1–1 provides a conceptual model of the relationship between the elements of cost and revenue for many large service firms, including the shrinking margins experienced by larger firms. The implications of this model are further borne out with the results of the profitability analysis depicted in Exhibit 1–2.

Experience Curve

The experience curve works differently in service companies than in industrial enterprises. As a rule, in manufacturing organizations with highly standardized products, unit costs decline about 15 percent with every doubling of production. When managed well, the experience curve offers competitive advantage to manufacturers that move quickly to build volume and share. Since service cannot be standardized, the experience curve does not benefit service companies directly by reducing unit costs. Instead, it improves service as people

EXHIBIT 1–1
The Typical Service Model Cost/Revenue Structure

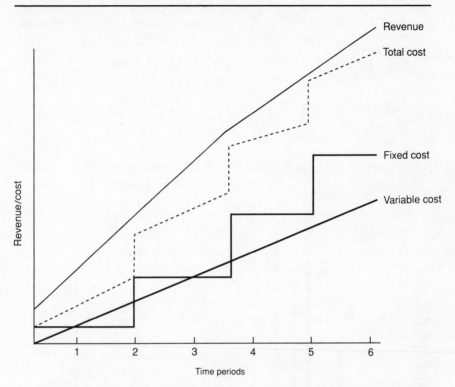

repeatedly perform both simple and complex tasks. Investment bankers, for example, become increasingly proficient with every financing they structure. Similarly, as a management consultant expands a client and project base, the more effective is the consulting. As quality improves, so does the value of service to the customer and, therefore, the price that the service can command.

The experience curve can yield competitive advantage to manufacturers through growth and share. "Learning by doing" can yield a competitive advantage for service companies if they involve employees directly in design and delivery of the service. The Mayo Clinic, for example, has achieved a sustained competitive advantage in medical services by encouraging its physicians to participate actively in designing services.

EXHIBIT 1–2
Profitability and Firm Size

Relative Profitability and Service Industry Growth

Industry	Industry Concentration	Relative Profitability
A Legal services	1.7	1.093
B Health services	3.2	1.014
C Personal services	5.2	1.018
D Consulting	8.9	1.151
E Equipment rental and leasing	11.6	1.128
F Engineering, architecture, and surveying	16.4	1.198
G Hotels, etc.	17.3	0.984
H Computer services	21.3	1.035
I Food stores	22.7	0.994
J Accounting	28.3	0.995
K Department stores	57.8	0.994

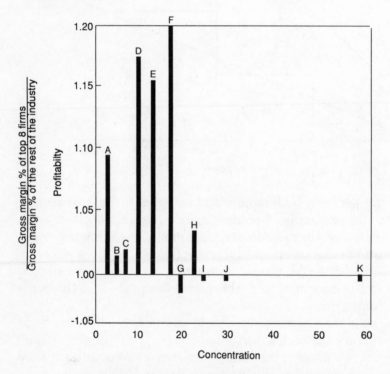

Concentration % = $\dfrac{\text{Receipts of the top 8 firms}}{\text{Industry receipts}}$

Source: *The Services Bulletin,* a newsletter of the Fischman-Davidson Center for the Study of the Service Sector. The Wharton School of the University of Pennsylvania 1 (Summer 1986), p. 1.

Growth, Size, and Share

Economies of scale and the experience curve tend to reward growth, size, and market share in manufacturing with improved profits. But, they do not similarly benefit service firms. Unless it is accompanied either by "first mover" advantages, where a "brand name" is swiftly established, or by gains in unit productivity—such as sales per employee or sales per square foot—growth in service companies tends to dilute earnings per share, earnings per professional, or other unit profitability.

In addition, size has little relation to profitability in service companies. In fact, size has often depressed profits. Large retailers are no more—and often less—profitable than smaller ones. Most large money-center banks and brokerage houses are not as profitable as regional banks and brokers. Insofar as size benefits service institutions, it does so indirectly by improving their image. Image enhancement can reduce corporate advertising costs in some markets and helps the firm attract and keep talented employees and clients.

Like growth and size, market share does not reward service firms with improved profits. As a rule, the profit margins of service firms with a larger share of their market are no better than the average margins of competitors in a given industry as shown in Exhibit 1–2.

Professor Gerald Faulhaber, of The Wharton School, has done extensive economic research on the service sector. In his role as director of the Fischman-Davidson Center for the Study of the Service Sector, Faulhaber produced the study of relative profitability and firm size depicted in Exhibit 1–2. The table at the top of Exhibit 1–2 contains a set of ratios that compare industry concentration (revenues of the largest eight competitors divided by total revenues for the industry) to the profitability (gross margins minus payroll) of the largest eight competitors divided by the profitability of the industry. The table reveals that industries with the highest concentration—department stores, accounting firms, food stores, etc.—are somewhat less profitable than industries where there is little concentration. The graph at the bottom of Exhibit 1–2 presents the same data in graphic form.

Market share among industrial organizations seems to correlate with profitability, and it is easier to measure because of the tangible nature of a product. Market share suggests a finite market and is therefore more relevant to products. Since services are variable, unpredictable, and infinite in their potential for meeting the consumer's changing needs, market share is more elusive in a service context and less relevant to services.

Introducing a Product or Service

Introducing a service into the market is usually riskier than launching a product. To determine its marketability, an industrial or consumer product may be tested, modified, or withdrawn. Moreover, a new market segment for an existing product can be developed using the experience gained from servicing current market segments with similar products. Services, on the other hand, cannot be treated the same way. Their marketability is hard to determine by sampling or other trial techniques. Consumers cannot try on or try out the service. They cannot return it if the quality does not meet expectations. A "money-back" guarantee or warranty is meaningless in a service setting. Even such a highly successful company as Federal Express learned this the hard way when it made the foray into electronic data transfer. To test the viability of its widely publicized Zap Mail service, Federal Express had to establish a national network. The failure of Zap Mail to catch on after it was launched cost Federal Express a reported $350 million after taxes.

To market a new service, service companies must rely on the trust, confidence, and good will of customers. For a service to be considered by a particular market, the firm must depend on previously established relationships and on customers' perceptions of value and quality. If the risk of introducing a service is greater than that of introducing a product, the risk of recovery is also greater. If a manufacturing company puts out an unacceptable product but meets its warranties, and swiftly corrects the problem, it can quickly regain its image of quality. Faced with a similar miscalculation, however, a service company may never repair its reputation for quality and reestablish the crucial bond of trust with customers.

Barriers to Entry

In the short run, barriers to entry seem lower in service companies than manufacturing companies, but in the long run, sustaining a service business may be more difficult. The traditional barriers available to industrial companies are not as available to service companies. These include: capital intensity, a proprietary technology, cost structures, industry standards, government regulation, tax policies, switching cost, trade barriers, and talent. Service companies that erect most of these barriers often find that they are temporary and ultimately ineffective. In recent years, many banks have discovered that while additional capital may be essential to survival, it is not a competitive barrier. Conversely, some regional investment banks and broker/dealers have avoided outside capital infusions and successfully competed against larger firms in their geographical areas. The only barriers to entry that work over the long run for service companies are:

- Their human resources.
- Their customer relationships.
- The power of their networks.

The human resource barrier deals with a service company's capacity to attract and keep more talented people than its competitors and to invest more intelligently in sharpening employee skills so that it can better serve customers. The second barrier to entry, customer relationships, works when a service company serves customers so well that it locks them into a long-term relationship, discouraging them from taking business elsewhere. The third barrier, network power, can be quite formidable. Blue Cross and Blue Shield, for instance, has built up such a powerful network of health care providers—including primary care hospitals, health maintenance organizations, preferred provider organizations, and secondary and tertiary health centers—that it is difficult for other insurance companies to duplicate that network or receive the pricing benefits that Blue Cross and Blue Shield enjoys in many markets. Federal Express and United Parcel Service largely owe success to their hub-and-spoke networks, which are so effective that it would be virtually impossible for any new company to break into the air-express business today.

Implementation of Change

A crucial but frequently overlooked difference between manufacturing and service companies is in how they implement change. Implementing change in service companies is more complex and riskier than in industrial companies.

Other things being equal, industrial and consumer products organizations can shift markets, change processes, and modify organizational structures more easily because the product can serve as the "engine" of change. Since the product functions as an integrating mechanism, executing change in a manufacturing firm does not necessarily require close interaction between persons who plan and persons who implement change. Product designs, specifications, and manufacturing processes can communicate to the work force what needs to be done and how to do it. Of course, involving the work force through programs like quality circles helps expedite change and improve quality. But, even worker participation programs succeed chiefly because they promote a greater organizational focus on the product.

Implementing any substantive change in a service firm hinges on other factors. The production and delivery of services are so people-intensive that successful change requires modifying the attitudes and behavior of every organizational member. A close interaction between the planners and executors of change is essential to achieve a consensus among everyone affected by the change. The need for modified attitudes, behavior, and a broad consensus calls for a higher degree of communication and involvement by senior managers. **In service companies, change is not done *to* people. Change is made *with* people.**

CONCLUSIONS

The differences between manufacturing and service companies outnumber similarities. The gaps between the two organizations are so great, in fact, that comparing them may seem futile. Yet, the product and manufacturing bias is so deeply rooted in U.S. business that the comparative exercise cannot be dismissed.

Despite the more prominent and growing role of the service sector in the economy, service companies have not yet earned the recognition and the distinctive conceptual focus that they deserve. Service managers continue to apply inappropriate planning models and strategies from manufacturing to their own service institutions. In so doing, they often dim the prospects of achieving competitive advantage. Sometimes they jeopardize their survival.

CHAPTER 2

THE TOOLS: A FRAMEWORK FOR STRATEGIC ANALYSIS

The enormous differences that distinguish a service from a product, as well as the enterprises that offer services remain largely unacknowledged. The American business community continues to use the concepts and strategic models of industry to analyze, plan, and manage service companies. The evidence overwhelmingly suggests that the tendency to view service companies in a framework derived from manufacturing endangers the health of the service sector. The use of product-oriented concepts and models makes it harder for service companies to secure a lasting competitive advantage in the tough global environment.

The misapplication of manufacturing experience to the service sector is understandable. Lacking any comprehensive research on service-sector management, corporate managers, scholars, and management consultants have resorted to manufacturing examples for guidance. As the last chapter showed, historically, business has not given the service sector much attention. As a result, service managers have not enjoyed the benefits that their manufacturing peers have reaped from the research and insights of eminent figures such as Frederick Taylor, Alfred Sloan, Henry Ford, Edward Deming, Peter Drucker, and others.

This chapter begins to fill the gap by providing some strategic tools and conceptual approaches that are an appropriate framework for strategic thinking in service companies. Some of these tools and approaches are new; others are not. Their value, however, lies not in their originality so much as in their combined application. The tools are:

- The **service life cycle,** which helps a service organization identify the criteria of competitiveness and appropriate strategies during its youth, maturity, and declining phases.
- The **client/customer service spectrum,** which helps a service organization develop or sharpen its market focus by defining what the organization is, who it serves, and the attributes of its clients or customers.
- The **creation of service value,** which helps a service organization focus service delivery at any point on the spectrum.
- The **service value chain,** which helps a service organization determine how to muster the resources it needs to implement the strategies it has adopted for competing at any point on the spectrum.

Although the service sector includes many different industries, as well as companies and business units of varying sizes, the tools can be applied broadly. Used carefully, the tools are no less relevant to fast food companies than investment banks, no less relevant to large multinational service companies than to small, regional service firms.

THE LIFE CYCLE

The most basic, yet frequently neglected tool is the **life cycle.** It is available to service companies no less readily than manufacturing companies. Although controversy surrounds the appropriateness of a biological analogy to human organizations, it is safe to say that companies, professions, and industries—like people—move through various phases of a life cycle (see Exhibit 2–1). Also, the phases of a life cycle are largely predictable and irreversible.

Each phase of an organization's life cycle is characterized by different behaviors. Strategies that are appropriate at one stage of the life cycle may not be appropriate at another stage.

EXHIBIT 2–1
Reality—The Emerging/Reemerging Life Cycle

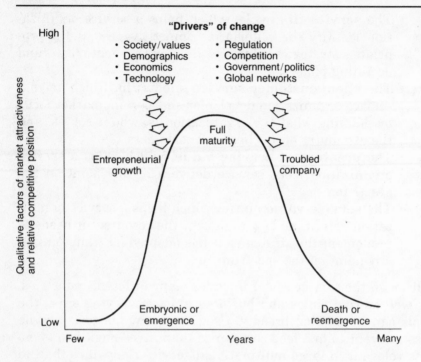

Early on, for example, a start-up or reemerging company is owner-managed, lean, dynamic, cash-hungry, and relatively unstructured. As the organization grows and matures, control becomes more elusive, prompting managers to functionalize, divisionalize, or institute matrix management systems. These new systems make it difficult for the organization to stay in close touch with its markets. To regain sensitivity to its markets, management often establishes strategic business units or other product-focused units. Left largely on their own, these units tend to drift apart, develop independent cultures, neglect cooperation, and generally make it harder to achieve corporate integration.

Having peaked in its life cycle, the organization finds further growth nearly impossible. Either markets are saturated or costs have risen so that prices cannot adequately cover them. Stagnation and decline occur. In the declining phase of its life cycle, the organization often becomes divorced from its markets, and management becomes more inwardly focused. Internal processes and corporate politics assume an overwhelming importance. An organizational "death-spiral" now looms as a possibility.

Again, like people who exert some control over their life cycles by changing their diets, exercise routines, and other aspects of their life-styles, organizations can retard their deterioration and decline by taking steps to prolong their vitality. But they can do even more because unlike people, organizations, professions, and industries are not born to die. Death is an avoidable feature of organizational life. To mitigate the severity of the aging process and, more importantly, to take advantage of competitors' maturity and deterioration, corporations can continually revitalize, reconfigure, and transform themselves. "Service organizations can't stand still just because they've coped with change once," says Earl H. Orser, the chairman and CEO of London Life Insurance Company in London, Ontario. "They can and must keep changing, moving, and reemerging." Rejuvenation feeds on strategy, and it presupposes a recognition of the organization's position on the life cycle.

Applying the Life Cycle

Despite its simplicity, the life cycle is an extremely useful tool. It is useful both as an indicator of where the company, profession, or industry has been, where it is, and where it is headed. Driven by both internal and external forces, the management of an organization can analyze its position on the life cycle to forecast both its future performance and future performance of competitors. The difficulty is reaching an internal consensus on these findings and, more importantly, on the actions that will prove most effective given these findings. This is why, as Chapter 5 shows, it is essential to develop a set of strategic conclusions regarding where an organization is on the life cycle.

The internal factors affecting an organization's life cycle are the vision and vitality of management and its ability to cope with change. This is more important in service companies than manufacturing because service companies are driven by people who, especially in the higher value-added services, are synonymous with the service.

The external factors affecting an organization's, profession's, or industry's life cycle include changes in the social, demographic, economic, financial, technological, political, and regulatory environments. Much has been written on environmental analysis or "environmental scanning," as some strategists call it. Service managers can avoid spending enormous time and money on pure research by turning to several readily available sources of information and analysis. In conducting research, however, managers should be aware that there is much more data available than there is useful information from which conclusions may be drawn. They should take special care to gather just enough data to help them position their organization, profession, or industry on the life cycle.

While the life cycle is an indispensable tool in the strategic analysis of any organization, it is especially relevant for service companies. The risk of neglecting the life cycle, in fact, is much greater for a service company than in manufacturing. Unlike manufacturers, many service companies have been heavily regulated historically. Except for the retail, food, and personal-care services, most major service industries—utilities, communications, transportation, banking, brokerage, insurance, legal services, accounting, and health care—have had to operate under the scrutiny of various state and federal agencies. Widespread regulation, in turn, has distorted the life cycles of services by substituting the politics of regulation for market reality.

Regulation has made many service companies, professions, and industries feel immune to the life cycle. With regulators replacing markets, service companies have not been pressured to respond to the environmental forces affecting the life cycle. The false protection that regulators have afforded service companies has fostered self-serving attitudes among service managers and a greater inward organizational focus than if companies had to compete in an unregulated marketplace.

This regulation mentality and the subsequent neglect of the life cycle have often prompted service companies to behave in self-destructive ways. While still in their growth phases, for example, many service companies and professions have sought to protect their gains by erecting artificial barriers including, among others, professional associations, professional standards, licensure and certification procedures, and continued or enhanced government regulation. Many of these barriers were created to protect the public but, in fact, they have predictably restrained trade or limited competition. The barriers have restricted the supply of services, raising prices to unsustainable levels.

Blinded to the life cycle, many service companies, professions, and industries have overlooked the likelihood that eventually regulations would be lifted and barriers dismantled. As a result, many service organizations have emerged in a less regulated and more competitive environment at a declining phase of their life cycle. The vast majority have been oblivious to this fact and are reeling from the consequences. Those companies that have recognized the new realities and their positions on the life cycle, however, have reemerged in more vital forms and gained substantive competitive advantage.

Real-Life Implications of the Life Cycle

Service companies, professions, and industries can incur significant risks by neglecting the life cycle. The following examples clearly illustrate those risks in several industries:

• The demise of fixed commissions and the introduction of negotiated commissions in the securities industry shook the economic structure of the traditional firms and spawned the discount brokerage industry. Both industries have now reached maturity: the traditional firms as new/merged entities, and the discount brokerage firms, as subsidiaries of full-service banks or insurance companies.

• The deregulation of interest rates threatened the commercial banking industry while providing strategic opportunities to banks that recognized their industry's life cycle and anticipated the change. Some banks have not yet recovered from the damage wrought by deregulation. Those that foresaw it—Citicorp, Bankers Trust, and BancOne, for example, have benefited from deregulation.

• Structurally high interest rates, the deregulation of banking, and slower economic and population growth have made traditional life-insurance services and the industry nearly obsolete. Their unrecognized position on the life cycle created new opportunities for niche players while forcing the larger insurance firms like The Prudential and Equitable to reemerge as full-service financial service institutions.

• By creating more efficient channels of distribution for personal lines, property, and casualty insurance and reducing costs, Allstate and State Farm jeopardized the American Agency System used by companies such as The Hartford, Fireman's Fund, Aetna, and Travelers. Had the large commercial companies recognized where they were on the life cycle, they might have done more to change their expensive distribution system.

• The rising costs of litigation have changed the economics of law firms as corporate clients have established and increasingly relied on in-house counsel while consumers meet their less sophisticated legal needs by frequenting the new retail chains of "storefront" law firms such as Jacoby & Meyers on the East Coast and Hyatt Legal Services on the West Coast.

• Rising costs and a maturing, stable market for the traditional services of public accounting firms prompted several firms to reemerge by diversifying into new areas. Arthur Andersen and Peat Marwick, for example, developed software, and Touche Ross developed a substantial general management consulting practice simultaneously with developing a focused information technology practice.

• The combined effects of deregulating the airline and bus industries changed the strategic position of transportation companies, like Greyhound, on their life cycles. Having recognized the change, Greyhound, for example, reemerged in a more competitive form as a market-driven passenger, package express, and charter transportation company. Greyhound chairman and CEO John Teets pays close attention to his industry's and company's changing position on the life cycle. "When I took over," John Teets says, "all the companies Greyhound had acquired were at the tail end of their life cycles. Some could be rejuvenated through strategy and others through changes in the economic structure of the industries of which they were a part."

THE CLIENT/CUSTOMER SERVICE SPECTRUM

The second and most important tool available to service companies is the **client/customer service spectrum** (See Exhibit 2–2). Among other things, the spectrum is invaluable in helping service companies determine what markets to serve and how to most effectively serve them. Variations of the spectrum have been used by service companies that have achieved a lasting competitive advantage.

The client/customer service spectrum is based on the premise that corporations and their business units range along a horizontal spectrum containing points that represent different market needs. How a company or business unit meets those needs—how it creates value—differs according to the entity's position on the spectrum.

The user of a service tends to be sophisticated and is referred to as a "client" rather than a "customer" at the left of the spectrum. The client's demand for unique solutions to complex problems—for what approaches "pure" service—makes the

EXHIBIT 2–2
Client/Customer Service Spectrum

Client ("pure" service)	Client/customer (service/product)	Customer ("product")
1	2	3
Client need: Unique solutions to complex problems	**Client/customer need:** Experience-based solutions to more routine problems	**Customer requirement:** Generic solutions to common requirements

professional who provides the service nearly indispensable to the client. The problems on the left of the spectrum are generally defined in close collaboration between the client and the professional. This end of the spectrum, therefore, includes such service businesses as medical care, executive financial counseling, international corporate law, international management consulting, specialty retail boutiques, executive search firms that recruit on retainer from clients, and gourmet restaurants (see Exhibit 2–3).

Finding and implementing the right solution to less complex problems is more important to service companies in the middle of the spectrum. Their problems are usually more technical, and solutions derive more from experience than problem-solving expertise. Examples are the prepackaged solutions offered by large software companies to clients with predefined problems. The service in the middle of the spectrum represents something between "pure" service and a "product." The user of the service falls somewhere between a "client" and a "customer." To a greater degree than at the left of the spectrum, the service here is defined by the client/customer—independent of the professional. Service companies that belong in this category are financial advisory services for individuals performed by financial intermediaries, local law firms, department stores, executive-search firms that recruit on a contingency basis, and "white tablecloth" restaurants.

At the extreme right of the client/customer service spectrum, the service becomes standardized; it nearly becomes a "product" that provides generic solutions to routine requirements. The service, however, is never a "pure" product because there is no such thing. The user of the product-like service is best thought of not as a "client" but as a "customer," who defines his needs and requirements with little if any assistance from the salesperson. Service companies that fall at this end of the spectrum include discount brokerage firms, retail banks, legal-service companies, discount stores, employment agencies, and fast-food chains.

The client/customer service spectrum does not reflect any value judgments upon the relative merits of different points along the spectrum. Moving left or right on the spectrum may

EXHIBIT 2–3
Examples of the "Served" Market

Client Need	Client/Customer Need	Customer Requirement
Pure Service	Service/Product	Product
International corporate attorneys	Local law firms	Legal service companies
Specialized medical treatment facilities	Hospitals, clinics, group facilities, individual practitioners	Emergency medical, outpatient treatment facilities
International management consulting firms	Consultant participants on client-project team	Request for proposal responses to predetermined problems
Executive financial counseling	Individual financial advisory services performed by financial intermediaries	Discount brokerage and retail banks
Expensive resorts and Spas	Middle-market inns	Low-priced motels
Executive search—noncontingent	Executive recruiting contingent	Employee agencies
Retail boutiques	Department stores	Discount stores
High-priced merchandise catalogs	Catalog showrooms	Electronic shopping
Gourmet restaurants	"White tablecloth" restaurants	Fast-food chains

33

be equally attractive alternatives with equally desirable results. What is important for service institutions, as the next
chapter shows, is establishing a clear strategic direction and
avoiding unintentional shifts toward what is sometimes a sur-
prise destination.

If, for example, a company is at a stage of its life cycle
where the market attractiveness of its particular service and
its competitiveness are declining, a look at the company and
the spectrum might reveal that the company was moving
toward the right, toward providing more generic solutions to
routine requirements. If this shift was not part of a conscious
direction, the company would unexpectedly find itself in a new
business it was not equipped for, resulting in new competitors
and, often, narrower margins. Slipping "down-scale" into a new
business the company is not equipped to be in is common.

In recent years, several law, public accounting, and management consulting firms have slipped "down-scale" by offering
prepackaged solutions. Often, in their efforts to grow faster,
increase the leverage of their professionals, and achieve economies of scale, service companies move toward the right of the
spectrum rather than rejuvenating themselves by shifting
toward the left, adding more value to their clients through
their professionals' expertise.

By carefully studying the client/customer service spectrum, management may also ask whether current capabilities
allow for a leftward move or whether the company should con-
solidate by moving toward the right, achieving whatever economies of scale may exist and competing primarily on price. An
evaluation of characteristics of both the markets that a service
company seeks to serve and of the organization's human resource capabilities allows management to establish a preliminary direction. This direction can be followed by detailed
strategies and tested for desirability of the outcome.

When using the client/customer service spectrum as a
strategic tool, it is important to note that business units often
have trouble focusing on more than one position on the spectrum. Business units serving the needs of many different
clients or customers with a combination of service and product-
like services are not as powerful as firms that focus their ef-

forts. This is not to say that a company should not serve multiple markets. But, when it does, it is usually best—as some banks, insurance companies, and other financial service firms have learned—to set up separate business units corresponding to the multiple points on the spectrum where the company wants to compete.

THE CREATION OF SERVICE VALUE

The third strategic tool available to service institutions is the concept of **value creation,** or how they meet the needs of markets they serve. This does not suggest that selecting a position on the client/customer service spectrum and developing the means for serving clients or customers are mutually exclusive. They are not. In fact, managers must avoid falling into the common trap of approaching the decision about which markets to serve as distinct from how they will serve them. Many commercial banks, for instance, have succeeded in matching and fine-tuning the needs of high net worth individual clients with their internal organizational capabilities. Banks have done so by treating the decision to serve these clients and how to serve them as a single, integrated process. The question underlying the process is "How can I muster the resources necessary to create value in a way that enables my company or business unit to most effectively serve the market I have chosen?"

Exhibit 2–4 combines the client/customer service spectrum with the chief means of creating value at three arbitrary points on the spectrum. The intersection of a given point on the spectrum and the activities used by the service provider to create value is referred to as the "power alley." This phrase captures the organization's ability to concentrate its resources on the activities it will perform to serve the given, focused market segment. By linking the needs of its clients or customers with the resources necessary to meet those needs, companies achieve a degree of focus with powerful effects. Conversely, companies lose this power when they become fuzzy or too general in their focus and response to markets.

EXHIBIT 2–4
The Creation of Service Value

Client ("pure" service)	Client/customer (Service/product)	Customer ("product")
△ 1	△ 2	△ 3

Client 25%	Client/Customer 20%	Customer 10%
		Interactive 10%
	Interactive 25%	Process 40%
Interactive 50%	Process 30%	
Process 15%	Supplier/ Vendor 25%	Source 40%
Provider 10%		

It is useful to regard the means of creating value as components of a service. Each of the components, in turn, is broken into activities, which form a "value chain." Success in any business, after all, hinges on performing in ways that ensure the success of clients or customers and suppliers. Companies that have achieved lasting competitive advantage have done so by focusing on and linking their activities with the activities that are important to their clients or customers and suppliers. It is this conscious linkage that makes the provider of the service indispensable to everyone with whom it does business.

Essential Service Components

Service institutions create value for themselves and their clients or customers through what might be visualized as a seamless pipe. This pipe might be viewed as four sections or service components:

- The client/customer component.
- The interactive component.
- The process component.
- The supplier (provider or source) component.

The means of creating value through these components differs at each point on the spectrum. The differences, in fact, account for the difficulty many service institutions have in serving diverse markets through generalized activities. The differences further explain why it is essential to focus not only on client or customer needs, but also on the specific activities required to meet those needs.

This is evident in the success enjoyed by focused or niche marketers like Toys"R"Us and The Limited, for example, as well as in the failures experienced by organizations that try to be all things to all people through one set of activities. The relative impact of each of the four components of service and the creation of value is illustrated by the relative weights assigned to each component in Exhibit 2–4.

The Client/Customer Component

This service component relates to activities performed by the service company's clients or customers, to the activities that are critical to the success of their organizations and to the well-being of individuals who work for them. The client or customer is a partner in the service delivery process, bringing different experiences, attitudes, emotions, needs, and problems to every situation. The client/customer component of the process represents those characteristics of the client or the customer which become an integral part of the entire process. Just as there are activities essential to the survival, competitiveness, and profitability of organizations, there are activities that are essential in satisfying the needs for security, self-esteem, and happiness of the individuals within organizations. The more vital the client's or customer's need, the greater the value a service company can create by meeting that need and therefore, the greater the opportunity for earning higher returns.

The value created through the client/customer component is highest on the far left of the spectrum, where the provider of the service is in a partner-like relationship with the client. The value created by the client/customer component declines as one moves toward the right of the spectrum, where the service company provides near-commodity services.

The Interactive Component

Ranging from the professional competence and personal demeanor of a physician at the extreme left of the client/customer service spectrum to the user-friendliness of an Automated Teller Machine at the right, the interactive component of service relates to the direct human or technical link connecting the company delivering the service to the client or customer.

The interactive component creates value for the user of the service by, at the same time, creating value for the service provider. Value is created through this component by ensuring that the component price is sufficient to cover its cost. Of all service components, the interactive one is the component companies can most effectively use to erect competitive barriers and increase switching costs. Examples are the attentiveness of Federal Express or United Parcel Service drivers; home banking; the family physician who knows the patient's medical history; or the lawyer on retainer. As Exhibit 2–4 shows, the interactive component is far more important in creating value at the left of the spectrum, where the interaction between the provider and user of the service is critical. The component declines in importance relative to the process component at the right of the spectrum, where the interaction between provider and user plays a smaller role.

The Process Component

The process component is a link between the interactive and supplier components. The process component consists of activities that support the problem-solving professionals on the left of the client/customer service spectrum. These activities include such things as microcomputer modeling, medical laboratory testing, and legal database research. The process component here is a necessary but insufficient basis of competition.

At the right of the spectrum, the process component is critical to the competitive success of the service company. Activities at this end include, for example, the effective personnel training programs and mechanization of McDonald's fast-food service, the computerization of H&R Block's tax preparation service, and the mechanized warehouse and distribution systems of large wholesale grocery distributors such as the Fleming Companies and medical supply companies such as Baxter. That the process component is a much more important basis of competition on the right of the spectrum does not mean that the quality of the component's activities is less important on the left. Quality is important regardless of position on the spectrum.

The Supplier Component

The supplier (provider or source) component creates value for the provider and user of the service through efficient sourcing. Again, as with the other components of service, the importance of this one varies across the client/customer service spectrum. Supplier-component activities on the left, which include the purchase of high quality and reliable computer equipment, or medical supplies, are important to the service provided. But, these activities acquire much greater competitive significance on the right. McDonald's relationship with the J. R. Simplot Company, its supplier of potatoes, allows McDonald's to sell customers excellent french fries. Retailers like The Gap, The Limited, and even diversified retailing giants like Sears, Roebuck & Co. gain competitive advantage by scouring the world for economical, high-quality merchandise.

CREATION OF VALUE AT THE ENTERPRISE LEVEL

Value must be created at the enterprise or corporate level if the entire organization is to exist over the long term. Exhibit

EXHIBIT 2–5
The Role of the Corporation

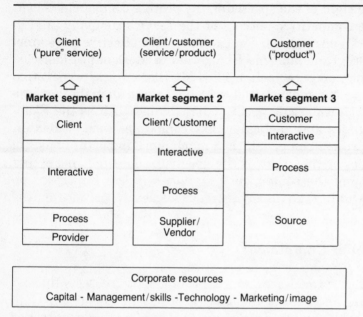

2–5 shows the notion of value from the client/customer service spectrum through a focus provided by the business units to the overall foundation of value, which is created at the corporate level.

The nature of the corporation's contribution to creating value at the business-unit level includes:

- Determining which markets to enter or leave.
- Sharing scare marketing and planning resources across business units, including the interbusiness networking of "products" and services.
- Allocating capital in both a traditional capital budgeting sense and from the risk/return viewpoint.
- Sharing and developing management skills.
- Developing nonbusiness-unit specific technology, including communications and data.

CHARACTERISTICS OF SERVED MARKETS

A service company creates value when it understands not only the relative roles of the four service components at different points on the spectrum, but the attributes of different markets it wants to serve. These attributes vary across the spectrum, from markets for "pure" service at the spectrum's far left to more product-like services at the extreme right (See Exhibit 2–6A for characteristics of served markets and Exhibit 2–6B for characteristics of value creation.)

Before looking at market characteristics, note that certain human attributes are so basic to all markets that they remain constant across the entire client/customer service spectrum. Ultimately, service companies are in the business of serving not markets and companies but people. The attitudes, emotions, needs, expectations, and behavior of the service company's clients or customers vary little from one end of the spectrum to the other.

Neither the absolute size of the market nor market share is important to the economics of the service company at the left of the spectrum. These markets tend to be fragmented and characterized by relatively few, highly sophisticated clients. The clients typically have considerable funds to spend on the service and seek the highest quality regardless of price. The markets at this end of the spectrum are further characterized by a high degree of client trust and confidence in the professional relationship.

As the service approaches product attributes and the process component becomes more important on the right of the spectrum, the markets are typically large and consumer-oriented with substantial concentration. Absolute size and market share are more critical to the provider's economics. The customers are cost conscious, and price is an important competitive factor. As always, quality is crucial because there is no price low enough to justify poor quality. Indeed, quality from the perspective of the client/customer is the fundamental basis of competition at all points on the spectrum.

EXHIBIT 2–6A
Characteristics of Served Markets

Client Need	Client/Customer Need	Customer Requirement
Pure Service	Service/Product	Product
Few clients	Relatively large market	Large consumer-type market
Fragmented markets	Some market concentration	Considerable market concentration
Absolute size and market share are not important	Absolute size and market share are somewhat important	Absolute size and market share are critical
Relative size may be important	Relative size is somewhat important	Relative size is critical
Large amounts of money to spend for service	Spending budgets tightly controlled	Very cost conscious
Sophisticated clients	Capable clients	Customer capability not an issue
High levels of client trust and confidence in the professional relationship	Moderate levels of client trust and confidence in the professional relationship	Integrity of the salesperson is always important
High demand for first-class service—quality regardless of the price	Quality is relative to competition	Value is important
International networking may be important	International capability not often an issue	International capability never an issue

EXHIBIT 2–6B
Characteristics of the Nature of Value Creation

Client Need	Client/Customer Need	Customer Requirement
Pure Service Characteristics	Service/Product Characteristics	Product Characteristics
Economies of scale less important	Economies of scale more important	Economies of scale very important
Price inelastic	Moderately price elastic	Very price elastic
High percentage variable costs	Lower percentage variable costs	High percentage fixed costs
Repeatability of exact solution less important than problem solving and implementation process—inductive logic	Finding and implementing the right solution is more important than the problem-solving process—deductive logic	Repeatability of the solution is critical
Highly important to a client's operation	Moderately important to a client's operation	Relatively unimportant to a client's operation
Unique solutions to common problems	Experience-based solutions to technical-type problems	Generic solutions to routine requirements
Problems defined through a "partnership" between the client and the professional	Service needs defined to a greater degree by the client independent of the professional	Product needs defined by the customer with little or no assistance from the provider/salesperson
High level of client dependence on the professional	Moderate level of client dependence on the professional	Little dependence by the customer on the provider/salesperson
Life cycle of the individual critical to success of service provider	Life cycle of the company and industry important	Life cycle of the product and industry critical

THE SERVICE-VALUE CHAIN

The **service-value chain** is useful for designing and executing service-sector strategies. The service-value chain maps out in detail the specific activities that service companies perform to create value for their clients or customers and suppliers. The chain represents a set of discrete tasks, functions, or activities which, when performed against even the toughest competitors, provides the basis for a lasting competitive advantage.

Exhibit 2–7, for example, illustrates the service-value chain for a typical commercial or investment bank. This service-value chain was created by a task force with which Touche

EXHIBIT 2–7

Investment Banking Service-Value Chain (Investment Banking Consists of Value-Added Services That Move Money From Investors of Capital to Users of Capital)

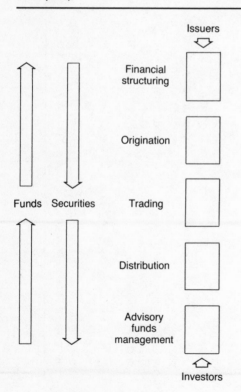

Ross was privileged to participate at Manufacturers Hanover Corporation, Investment Banking Group. The task force was chaired by Douglas E. Ebert, sector executive vice president. Working within the context of the client/customer service spectrum, and using the major components of the creation of service value, Exhibit 2–7 depicts the flow of securities from borrowers through the major activities that the Investment Banking Group performed in creating value for the ultimate investor. Of course, the flow of funds could be tracked back through the chain to the borrower. While this version of the service-value chain is highly conceptual, and detailed activities were later developed, the purpose included a framework for competitive analysis that led to a set of meaningful strategic conclusions and a framework for developing an organizational structure for the group. The Investment Management Group, as a business unit, has changed its position on the life cycle from a traditional commercial bank to a fast-moving, high-growth, profitable investment bank.

In a more generalized use of the service-value chain, depicted in Exhibits 2–7 and 2–8, if bank management determined that the bank could perform competitively, the bank could perform all activities in the service-value chain. If management determined that it could not perform all activities competitively, the bank could "network," syndicate, or otherwise funnel the activity through other institutions that demonstrated a competitive advantage in performing the given activity. Exhibit 2–9 is an example of a competitive analysis worksheet, which uses the service-value chain to provide an analytical framework for comparing the strengths and weaknesses as well as the cost structures of competitors—in this case, commercial firms or investment banks are shown.

Exhibit 2–10 is an example of a service-value chain for the health-care industry. This service-value chain was created by a task force led by William E. Flaherty, president and CEO of Blue Cross and Blue Shield of Florida, Inc. This service-value chain depicts the flow of a variety of health-care and financing services from the provider component of the creation of service value through to the patient, and it tracks the flow of funds from their source back through the chain to various activities

EXHIBIT 2–8
Investment Banking Service-Value Chain

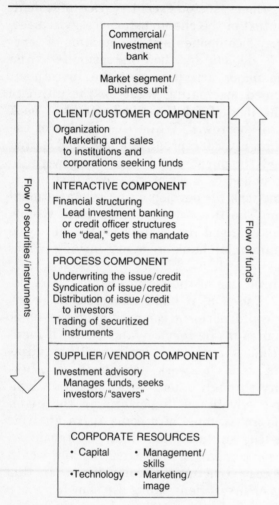

that created the value. Blue Cross and Blue Shield of Florida, under Bill Flaherty's leadership, has reemerged on its service life cycle from a traditional indemnity insurer to the dominant player in the newly formed Florida market for managed health care.

EXHIBIT 2-9
Competitive Analysis Worksheet Commercial/Investment Bank

Component of the Service	Point on the Client/Customer Service Spectrum *Market segment/business unit value chain*	Competitive Assessment/Fact Base					Conclusions *What our firm must do to achieve sustainable competitive advantage*
		Our firm	Competitors				
			A	B	C	D	
Client/Customer	Origination Marketing Sales	Basis of competition Strengths/Weaknesses					Build on strengths Overcome weaknesses
Interactive	Financial structuring Investment/banker Credit officer	Basis of competition Strengths/Weaknesses					Build on strengths Overcome weaknesses
Process	Underwriting syndication Distribution Trading	Basis of competition Strengths/Weaknesses					Build on strengths Overcome weaknesses
Supplier/Vendor	Investment advisory	Basis of competition Strengths/Weaknesses					Build on strengths Overcome weaknesses
Corporate Resources •Capital •Technology	•Management Skills •Marketing/Image	Basis of competition Strengths/Weaknesses					Build on strengths Overcome weaknesses

EXHIBIT 2–10
Health-care Industry Service-Value Chain

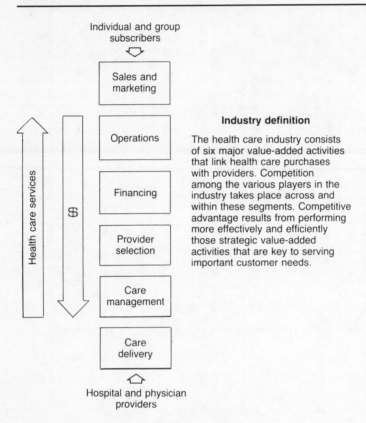

Industry definition

The health care industry consists of six major value-added activities that link health care purchases with providers. Competition among the various players in the industry takes place across and within these segments. Competitive advantage results from performing more effectively and efficiently those strategic value-added activities that are key to serving important customer needs.

CONCLUSIONS

Service companies can create value in various ways. Competitive success derives from many different factors, depending on where the service institution is in its life cycle and where it is located on the client/customer service spectrum. While growth, size, and market share vary in relative importance according to the markets the service company seeks to serve, nowhere on the spectrum are any of these manufacturing strategies applicable to service companies that want to achieve a lasting competitive advantage.

Whatever the merits of growth, size, market share, and other strategies for industrial companies, service companies must look to other strategies. This chapter has introduced four analytical tools designed to help service companies forge their distinctive strategies. Locating the service company, profession, or industry on the life cycle, the first tool, is essential. The second tool, the client/customer service spectrum, helps service companies achieve a market focus. Value creation through the four components of service helps service companies focus the delivery of services at any given point on the spectrum. This, in turn, leads to the fourth tool, the service-value chain, which helps identify activities that directly correspond to the ways in which service companies mobilize the resources necessary to execute their strategies. As evident in subsequent chapters, it is only through the combined use of these tools and the integration of the underlying processes that a service company can begin to design and execute strategies that help achieve a sustained competitive advantage.

CHAPTER 3

MISSING: A STRATEGIC DIRECTION

Forging a strategic direction is the first step in the process of strategic thinking. Moreover, research and consulting experience suggests that strategic direction is an essential ingredient for a sustained superior performance. Specific strategies and other activities associated with strategic management and planning are meaningless without a prior sense of strategic direction. Although this observation is no less true of service companies than manufacturing firms, service companies often neglect the importance of strategic direction. The analytical tools introduced in Chapter 1—the service life cycle, the client/customer service spectrum, the creation of service value, and the service-value chain—are essential in helping service managers establish a strategic direction. The viability of the chosen strategic direction(s), in turn, can be tested during the strategic assessment process, which is detailed in Chapter 4.

DEFINING STRATEGIC DIRECTION

One begins to define a business's strategic direction by answering two questions:

- To whom does the service firm sell what?
- How does the business balance the needs of the chosen markets with the capabilities of the organization?

These questions presuppose another question, the answer to which defines the business. That question is, "What business or businesses are we in?" If these questions seem simple, it suffices only to recall Theodore Levitt's celebrated *Harvard Business Review* article, "Marketing Myopia."[1] Among other things, the article pointed out that U.S. railroad companies died because they viewed themselves as being only in the railroad business rather than in the transportation business.

If, for example, an organization was at a state in its service life cycle where its viability was in question, a strategic direction would help it reemerge in a more viable form. Strategic direction provides the driving force of change, and the basis for a long-term commitment. It can further provide the common language with which the organization communicates, as well as the framework and policies for testing and establishing specific strategies. Strategic direction allows for a management style characterized by greater leadership and less control, a style that is well-suited to service companies.

STRATEGIC DIRECTION VERSUS VISION

Corporate vision is often confused with the notion of strategic direction. While vision and direction do share a market–customer focus, the strategic direction(s) of successful service companies often grow out of a corporate vision. However, the two notions are quite different, as shown in Exhibit 3–1.

The elusiveness of "vision" and the difficulties that business scholars, journalists, and managers typically encounter when they try to define vision are no reflection on its importance. The experience of some of the most successful service companies, in fact, suggests that a broad vision of purpose articulated at the corporate level is often a prerequisite to formulating strategic direction for the business as a whole and/or strategic directions for each business unit. Like strategic direction, therefore, a vision is an essential component of the entire strategic thinking process. Corporate vision is important as a

---

[1]Theodore Levitt, "Marketing Myopia," *Harvard Business Review* 53, no. 5 (September-October 1975), pp. 26–48. Copyright © 1975 by the President and Fellows of Harvard College. All rights reserved.

EXHIBIT 3–1
A Prescription for Success

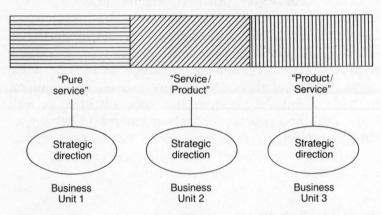

VISION STATEMENT

At which of the points along the client/customer
service spectrum do we/will we compete?

"Pure service"   "Service/Product"   "Product/Service"

Strategic direction   Strategic direction   Strategic direction

Business Unit 1   Business Unit 2   Business Unit 3

rallying point for an organization, serving as a catalyst for bringing the various divisions, subsidiaries, subsidiaries' divisions, or business units together in an integrated whole. A vision statement sets the tone for the service company, and it establishes a basis for the strategic direction(s) of the business units. "We constantly test the direction of each of our units against the corporate vision, which the heads of those units agree to," says Robert Winters, chairman and CEO of The Prudential.

Rather than redefining vision, it is more effective to cite some examples. Chairman Robert Brennan's corporate vision for Sears, Roebuck & Co. (see Exhibit 3–2) reads, in part:

> "Sears, Roebuck & Co., a family of diversified businesses, is the leader in providing and distributing quality products and services to consumers. We will engage in those commercial opportunities that leverage the distinctive capabilities of our existing businesses.
>
> We are committed to our most valued asset, our reputation for integrity.
>
> We dedicate ourselves to the principle that serving the customer is of prime importance."

EXHIBIT 3–2
Our Corporate Vision (The Sears, Roebuck and Co. Mission Statement)

Sears, Roebuck and Co., a family of diversified businesses, is the leader in providing and distributing quality products and services to consumers. We will engage in those commercial opportunities that leverage the distinctive capabilities of our existing businesses.

We are committed to our most valued asset, our reputation for integrity.

We dedicate ourselves to the principle that serving the customer is of prime importance.

We strive to provide our shareholders with a foundation for consistent and profitable investment growth. Our attractiveness to investors will be enhanced by the additional value created through our family of companies' coordinated activities.

We will manage ourselves as strong, decentralized business groups reporting to the Chairman of the Board. In their commitment to further objectives consistent with approved plans and the overall direction of the corporation, our groups will be supported by an efficiently structured corporate organization.

We will be a low cost provider, managing with efficiencies of scale, building upon a foundation of competitive cost advantages, and maximizing the productivity of resources which contribute directly to serving our customers.

We will allocate resources among our enterprises based upon an evaluation of their long-term relative profitability and the financial goals established by the corporation. We will maintain an overall capital structure which is stable, cost efficient and which provides an appropriate balance between financial leverage and business risk.

We will develop and distribute proprietary products and services when our reputation and skills add value and provide the opportunity to achieve greater profitability.

Our commitment to strategic planning is integral to managing our businesses and thinking long term.

We will be a leader in developing innovative applications of proven technology.

We will provide all employees—regardless of their sex, race, age, religion, disability or ethnic background—with an environment in which to maximize their potential and their contribution to our success, and we will see that they share in that success in meaningful ways.

We will faithfully fulfill our social and citizenship responsibilities.

We will communicate with customers, employees, shareholders, governments and the general public with the company's traditional devotion to integrity in order to enhance our reputation, advance company goals, and clarify company policy and activities.

Source: "Our Corporate Vision," Sears, Roebuck and Co., with commentary by Edward A. Brennan, Chairman and Chief Executive Officer, Senior Management Planning Forum, June 1986.

Chairman Robert Winters has a vision statement for The Prudential (see Exhibit 3–3). The statement begins:

> "The Prudential is, and will remain, the No. 1 insurance company in America. Leading with this strength, we will become the No. 1 financial services company in this market and a leader in global financial services."

> We will achieve this goal by enhancing our core businesses, and by entering related businesses that either reinforce our core businesses or provide superior returns. We will actively explore global markets and will enter those where we can leverage our strengths."

Later on in his vision statement, Winters lays more of a groundwork for strategic direction. "We will be aggressive and market-driven," he says. "We will operate through distinct business units, targeting specific market segments with coordinated strategies."

Few service executives have articulated the relationship between corporate-level and business-unit visions and the strategic directions that flow from them more effectively than Walter Wriston, the former chairman of Citicorp. In a speech entitled "The Citi of Tomorrow: Today"—delivered to the Bank and Financial Analysts Association in New York in 1984—his formulation was so effective that his comments deserve quoting at length. With regard to corporate vision, Wriston said:

> As a result of a study completed in 1967, we formed a bank holding company to permit us to broaden both our geographic and product base. We defined our business not as a United States commercial bank with branches abroad but rather as a global financial services enterprise with the United States as our home base.

Wriston then translates that overarching vision into specific vision for each of Citicorp's five major business units. He referred to them as the five I's: the institutional bank, the investment bank, the individual (consumer) bank, insurance, and information. Regarding the individual bank, for example, he said, "As we think ahead about the future of the individual bank, I am reminded of our model for the consumer business. We en-

EXHIBIT 3–3
Vision (The Prudential Vision Statement)

The Prudential is, and will remain, the No. 1 insurance company in America. Leading with this strength, we will become the No. 1 financial services company in this market and a leader in global financial markets.

We will achieve this goal by enhancing our core businesses, and by entering related businesses that either reinforce our core businesses or provide superior returns. We will actively explore global markets and will enter those where we can leverage our strengths.

Today, we serve our clients through four core businesses:

Individual	Institutional
Insurance	Asset Management
Investments	Employee Benefits

Our strategies will build on the competitive strengths that distinguish The Prudential:

Our name and reputation, based on public recognition of our integrity and rock-solid foundation;

Multiple distribution channels, including the largest full-time sales force in financial services;

Financial size and the skills to capitalize on it; and

A range of products and services that gives our clients the advantages of choice and our company the benefits of diversification.

We will be aggressive and market-driven. We will operate through distinct business units, targeting specific market segments with coordinated strategies. We will emphasize accountability and reward accomplishment, while stressing ethical behavior. We will continue Prudential's tradition of social responsibility.

As a mutual company, we will act always in the long-term interests of our policyholders.

We will measure our performance by balanced growth among earnings, revenue and market share, and by our competitive ranking in these measures.

Our greatest assets are our clients and our people who serve them. We are proud of both, and of our tradition of providing quality, acting with integrity, and helping our clients meet their financial objectives.

---

vision a world of 35 million Citicorp customers producing earnings of $30 per customer." Regarding the investment bank, Wriston said, "As cross-border lending slows, developing and industrial countries alike will be forced to develop their indigenous capital markets. Citicorp's investment bank intends to fulfill a leadership role in this effort." Regarding the insurance business, Wriston said:

> "Insurance is a natural adjunct to our consumer business, particularly when one considers the current outmoded and expensive agency method of distribution that permeates the industry . . . we are already a major factor in credit insurance and we intend to become a factor in the insurance business worldwide . . . we will initially engage in a strategy of commercial insurance distribution, as opposed to underwriting, as the legal barriers fall in the United States. We will ultimately become an underwriter for target markets focusing on financial guarantees and the funds flow side of the business . . ."

Returning to corporate vision, Wriston concluded his speech as follows:

> "The structure of "I" to the fifth power corporation may change, but the principles will remain. We have identified our businesses and we are working to place each of them in a class by themselves. These businesses will prosper as we further the five values that have formed the Citicorp culture for the past twenty years: integrity, a passion for customer service, a truly decentralized operating network overlaid by a central accounting and control system, visible rewards for innovation and an empathy for our people."

Neglecting Strategic Direction

In most service companies, particularly in less successful ones, strategic direction is often neglected. As the title of this chapter suggests, a strategic direction is missing either because the companies have not had a strategic direction from the start or the strategic direction has been lost.

There are a number of reasons for the lack of strategic direction(s). One reason is that as service companies move through various stages of their life cycles, their original focus or strategic direction gets lost. This is a frequent symptom of aging in a mature or maturing company. New generations of professional managers fail to rekindle the entrepreneurial fires that lit the original focus or direction upon which the company was built. As organizations become "divisionalized," departmentalized, functionalized, or otherwise compartmentalized along lines that distance the company from its clients or customers, the direction providing the original drive is lost. The entire organization typically falls victim to mixed signals regarding its purpose and what is important.

Expansion through mergers and acquisitions is another reason many companies have lost their strategic direction. Pursued in the quest for scale and market share, mergers and acquisitions have tended to blur the direction of companies that have acquired, or merged with other companies. Even in the few instances where service companies have merged successfully with other companies, they have lost some strategic direction. It was not until Herbert Wexler properly integrated The Limited, Lerner's, Victoria's Secret, Lane Bryant, Contempo, and other acquisitions, for example, that the group achieved a viable new strategic direction at both the corporate and business-unit levels.

Finally, the globalization and proliferation of services have prompted many service companies to become "all things to all people." In these companies, through one or several business units, the original market–customer focus has become so diffused that the strategic direction may be missing and permanently lost. One needs to look only as far as the Appendix of this book to see organizations that have an unfavorable Sustainable Performance Index (SPI). The Appendix identifies organizations across a wide range of *The Fortune Service 500* industries, and includes firms that are struggling with a direction.

The analytical tools and techniques described in the previous chapter are designed to help service managers establish a strategic direction that will lead to lasting competitive advantages for start-up and reemerging companies. For all that is written about strategic planning, little has been said about the need to establish a strategic direction. Strategy is a futile exercise in data gathering and analysis without a tentative prior sense of strategic direction, without some notion about "what the business can be."

ESTABLISHING A STRATEGIC DIRECTION: SELECTING A POINT ON THE SPECTRUM

The process of strategic thinking begins with a hypothetical strategic direction. The viability of the direction is then tested throughout the strategic assessment process (Chapter 4) and the strategic conclusions that the assessment generates (Chapter 5). The conclusions might confirm the direction that the company or business unit chose to follow. Alternately, the conclusions might show that the hypothetical direction does not work for the company or business unit, which forces managers to change direction.

A strategic direction can be established by selecting a point on the client/customer service spectrum congruent with management's preliminary decision about what the business can become. Selecting a point on the spectrum, where management chooses to compete, provides a focus to the data gathering necessary during the strategic assessment. More importantly, selecting a point gives everyone within the company the importance of a focus or direction as a basis for thinking strategically about the organization as a whole.

By selecting a point on the spectrum, the service company identifies the market it has chosen to serve along with the activities necessary for creating value in that market. In searching for a strategic direction, for example, the chairperson of a large, international executive recruiting firm recently asked us, "Tell me how high is up. How large can this business become, what are our obstacles to growth, and are we constrained in any way by the size of the market or by our competition?" Based on the point of the client/customer service spectrum where the chairperson's firm chose to compete, the characteristics of the market segment served, and the recruiting firm's capabilities, we hypothesized that there were no constraints on the growth of that firm except for its continued ability to attract and keep high-caliber recruiters. The hypothesis was tested during the strategic-assessment phase of the process and later confirmed by the strategic conclusions. The strategic direction that emerged was having the firm expand its retainer-based recruiting business at the high end of the market.

In another example, a small management consulting firm selected a point on the spectrum where it would compete with the large, multinational consulting firms. This hypothetical strategic direction was subsequently changed when the firm came to recognize that the caliber of its consultants was not as high as the caliber of the consultants at the larger, competing firms and that its client base looked very different from theirs.

Finding an appropriate strategic direction often involves a delicate balancing act that requires matching the capabilities of the service company with the needs of the particular market it seeks to serve. The various business units of both Sears, Roebuck & Co. and The Prudential went through this exercise. After being acquired by Sears, Dean Witter Reynolds, for example, agreed that Sears' own corporate vision was essentially a consumer vision. To fulfill that vision and take advantage of Sears' customer base, Dean Witter management first thought that it could continue to serve both retail and institutional customers with a wide variety of services. When this began to dilute the firm's focus and market power, management decided to shift its entire focus to the consumer, to serve them through a first-rate retail brokerage operation, and to deemphasize some institutional business.

The importance of setting a strategic direction as a basis for developing and implementing workable strategies is clear. What is less obvious is the usefulness of setting strategic direction for internal communication in a service company. To a greater extent than manufacturing strategies, successful service strategies hinge on the commitment of persons who execute the strategy. Corporatewide commitment is best achieved through a wide consensus among management levels and employees. Setting strategic direction(s) helps launch the consensus-building process by bringing together corporate-level and business-unit managers to discuss what the organization and its parts are about, alternative visions, and strategic direction.

ESTABLISHING A STRATEGIC DIRECTION: SELECTING BUSINESS UNITS

Another critical component of a strategic direction is selecting the appropriate business units. The careful selection of business units is more important to service companies than manufacturing units. Despite their awareness of markets, manufacturing companies tend to focus on the tangible product and on the application of the product across many markets. Independent business units designed to serve specific markets do not usually appear in manufacturing companies until later in their life cycles, after functionalization has occurred.

To operate effectively, service companies, on the other hand, must focus their efforts on the clients or customers who constitute their markets. This focus is best achieved in business units uniquely dedicated to serving specific markets. The earlier in its life cycle the service company organizes these units, the more successful the company.

Once service managers have arrived at a hypothetical strategic direction, targeted a point on the spectrum, and established the means of creating value at that point, the selection of business units becomes essential. After all, clients or customers are most effectively served and strategies are most effectively implemented through business units that face directly against each market. Moreover, the individuals responsible for executing strategies and for serving clients or customers are found in the business units and not on some corporate staff. Although value in a service company is also created at the corporate level, all the revenue, and ideally most costs, are concentrated in the business units.

Service companies that target multiple markets at various points on the client/customer service spectrum, as Exhibit 3–1 shows, should be viewed as following multiple strategic directions, one direction for each of its units. What service managers call the "business unit" does not matter. The business unit might be called an SBU, a planning unit, a profit center, a revenue center, a cost center, a division, or a subsidiary. What is important for service companies establishing a strategic direction is the link between the direction the company has chosen and the organizational unit it charges with implementing the direction.

The corporate vision and overall direction of Sears, Roebuck & Co. (Exhibit 3–2) finds more specific expression in the strategic directions for each of Sears' business units, which include: the Sears Merchandise Group, Allstate Insurance, Coldwell Banker, and Dean Witter Reynolds. Similarly, for The Prudential (Exhibit 3–3), which has a specific strategic direction—congruent with its corporate vision—for each of its business units or groups. These include: Individual Insurance, Group Insurance, Pension Asset Management, Property and Casualty, Pru Re-Insurance, Pru Investments, and Prudential Bache.

It is assumed in this book that all activities associated with strategic management are implemented at the business-unit level. This simplifying assumption allows the book to follow the strategic-management process without the complications that arise when dealing with organizations that serve multiple markets through a single business unit or with organizations that serve a single market through multiple business units.

For a business unit to operate successfully within its organization, it must meet certain criteria. These criteria are summarized impressively by Steve Brandt in *Strategic Planning in Emerging Companies*.[2] According to Brandt, the business should:

- Lend itself readily to the collection of data about market opportunities.
- Be reasonably comparable to other planning units for decision-making purposes.
- Facilitate implementation once decisions are reached about the mission of the unit in the company's future.

A final criterion is the need for business units to be fluid and flexible, to change when necessary in line with changes in the

---

[2]Steven C. Brandt, *Strategic Planning In Emerging Companies* (Reading, Mass.: Addison-Wesley, 1982).

needs of markets served by the business units. The natural tendency to resist change, especially in mature service companies, makes this a tough criterion to meet and, therefore, all the more important to recognize.

Service managers must be aware of two potential problems that have plagued the selection of business units. One problem is the integration of units. A lack of coordination among business units makes it impossible for the individual units to benefit from the image and reputation of the whole company. A balance between the autonomy and independence of each business unit and the coordination among them is essential to the enterprise's overall success.

The other problem relates to human resources. It is sometimes difficult to balance the needs of the business unit's market and the unit's human resource capabilities. A fine balance must be struck between the desire among many service managers to be generalists and serve markets of their choosing on the one hand and the business unit's need for functional specialization and true market responsiveness. This human resource problem affects not only the selection of business units but, later on, the creation of unit-specific strategies.

Service companies that have successfully selected a business unit include the following examples:

• To avoid confusing its existing market and deploy its resources more effectively and efficiently, the Robert Half employment agency has formed a separate business unit to provide temporary employment services. This business unit does not have to face a group of competitors new to Robert Half. As a result, the business unit has designed its resources and capabilities specifically to compete against other firms in that market.
• To survive the homogenization of the financial-services industry, many large commercial banks are moving away from the tendency to organize along traditional functional specialties. Instead, banks are increasingly serving their markets through independent but coordinated business units. The trust departments of these banks, for example, have divided their functional organizations and introduced market-driven business units designed to serve high net worth individuals, sports

and entertainment personalities, business executives, and entrepreneurs. These separate units, which were created from the old trust department, now compete with brokerage firms, insurance companies, and personal financial advisors.

• Many public accounting firm executives have recognized that they can continue to grow only by implementing strategies that target the separate and distinct markets they serve and by establishing business units that serve those markets. As a result, some independent public accounting firms have regrouped their old auditing, tax, and management consulting departments into market-driven business units designed specifically to serve specialty markets such as health care, small businesses, and financial services.

THE ROLE OF THE CORPORATE LEVEL

The focus on the business unit and the importance of its role in establishing a strategic direction and in the overall strategic management process should not minimize the corporate level role in creating value for a service company (Exhibit 2–5). Although most business units can operate fairly autonomously, they must get help from the efficient allocation of resources at the corporate level. Resources that are more efficiently allocated at the corporate level—of a service company no less than a manufacturing company—include capital, management skills, technology, and marketing.

As a rule, service companies create little value when they take a portfolio approach, leaving each business unit on its own. In these instances, it is never clear why the business units need the corporation. The role of the corporate level becomes clearer, however, when it seeks to improve the competitive position of each business unit, when it ensures that there is enough coordination and communication among the business units so that the overall company exceeds the sum of its parts.

The remainder of this book builds on the assumption that business units have been formed along market lines or that they will be formed based on the conclusions drawn from the strategic assessment process.

PART II

"WHERE ARE WE?"

OVERVIEW OF THE SECTION

This section could be titled, "A Strategic Assessment." Such a term—*assessment*—connotes two main themes:

- *How* does an institution stand relative to the toughest competition at each point on the client/customer service spectrum where it chooses to compete?
- *What* does an institution have to do to achieve sustainable competitive advantage?

The issues of how to start are established along five major dimensions; the issues of what to do to build on our strengths and overcome our weaknesses are established in the phrase entitled strategic conclusions.

The strategic conclusions phase of the strategy-management process, in many respects, is the most emotionally difficult for managers to face because it involves "looking into the mirror" and seeing ourselves with the same harsh reality that the world sees as it looks at us and our relative competitive performance. For this reason, it is also the most critical step in the process, because it is from this self-appraisal of what must be done that appropriate strategies are designed. If the conclusions are not right, there is no reason to expect that appropriate strategies will emerge.

PART II
"Where Are We?" (Versus Competition)

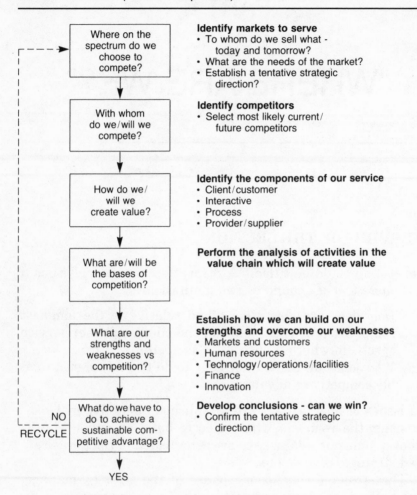

Identify markets to serve
- To whom do we sell what - today and tomorrow?
- What are the needs of the market?
- Establish a tentative strategic direction?

Identify competitors
- Select most likely current/ future competitors

Identify the components of our service
- Client/customer
- Interactive
- Process
- Provider/supplier

Perform the analysis of activities in the value chain which will create value

Establish how we can build on our strengths and overcome our weaknesses
- Markets and customers
- Human resources
- Technology/operations/facilities
- Finance
- Innovation

Develop conclusions - can we win?
- Confirm the tentative strategic direction

As John W. Teets at The Greyhound Corporation points out, "We concluded that we had the luxury of time to restructure both the corporation and its subsidiaries. The companies were strong enough to permit restructuring, however, we had inherited a "mixed bag," which, over time, must be rationalized if we are to survive." In the case of Greyhound, strategic conclusions formed the basis for establishing a competitive strategy for each of the Greyhound businesses.

The confirmation of the strategic direction hypothesis translates the *what* required to achieve competitive success to *how* such success will be attained. This confirmation sets the stage for Part III—Where Are We Going and How Do We Get There?

CHAPTER 4

A STRATEGIC ASSESSMENT: MARKETS AND CUSTOMERS, HUMAN RESOURCES, TECHNOLOGY–OPERATIONS– FACILITIES, FINANCE, AND INNOVATION

THE STRATEGIC-ASSESSMENT PROCESS

Having decided on a hypothetical strategic direction by choosing a point on the spectrum, having established the means of creating value at that point, and having created the business unit that will implement the strategic direction, successful companies undertake a strategic-assessment process. This process, which is also called an analysis of relative competitive position, enables companies to determine the viability of the chosen strategic direction. A strategic assessment is a diagnostic evaluation of how the business unit compares with competitors. The process helps identify the business unit's strengths and weaknesses relative to its competitors at the given point on the spectrum. Based on the conclusions derived from the assessment—the subject of the next chapter—service managers can decide either to pursue the direction they have chosen or to change it.

The need for strategic assessment is not distinctive to service companies. Most successful manufacturing companies have long engaged in the process; but, it is especially important for service companies. The risk of neglecting the strategic-assessment process is greater for service companies than for manufacturing companies. There are two reasons for this; one is that the need for a change in strategic direction is frequently less evident in service companies. If a product does not sell, the cause is usually obvious. It may have to do with changing consumer tastes, quality, or price. The reasons for the lagging sales of a less tangible service, however, are more varied and less immediately obvious.

The other reason for the greater risk of neglecting the strategic-assessment process in service companies relates to the differences in how change is implemented. When a manufacturing company needs to change its strategic direction, the change can be executed successfully with relatively few people accepting the need for change. In most service companies, however, it is impossible to implement change successfully without a broad consensus on the need for change. The strategic-assessment process creates an opportunity for everyone in a service company to participate in the data gathering and analysis and, therefore, to internalize the need for change.

RISKS OF NEGLECTING THE STRATEGIC-ASSESSMENT PROCESS

In the service sector, the strategic-assessment process has been observed more in the breach. Two service companies that pursued the strategic-assessment process and derived enormous benefits from it are Bankers Trust and Toys "Я" Us. Twelve years ago, Bankers Trust assessed their competitive position relative to other New York money-center banks. Their assessment yielded the conclusion that the bank could not compete effectively on all fronts against other banks, least of all against Citicorp, which enjoyed a larger infrastructure and capital base. Based on the conclusions of its lengthy assessment, Bankers Trust management decided it could achieve a lasting competitive advantage. One area was merchant banking, where management knew they could work off their impressive corporate client base. Another area was trust banking, where

Bankers Trust had distinctive strengths. Had Bankers Trust not gone through this process, it likely would not be as successful as it is today.

In the early 1980s, Toys "Я" Us managers went through a similar strategic-assessment process. Having combed through extensive economic and market data, management concluded that while its pricing, siting, marketing, and merchandising strategies were sound, there were limits on the company's ability to continue rapid growth. As a result, it used its sound approach and brand name to diversify into children's clothes through a new venture called Kids "Я" Us. Despite the number of first-class competitors Kids "Я" Us faces, the venture has paid off.

For every successful service company that has recognized the need for a strategic assessment, however, there are scores of companies—indeed entire industries—that have neglected the process, often with unhappy results. A case in point is the thrift industry. With few exceptions, the nation's savings banks and savings and loan associations never bothered analyzing their position relative to competitors in financial services. The thrifts failed to do this despite foreseeable deregulation and the effects that deregulation and a changing economy would have on the thrifts' competitive position. The information currently available to the thrifts was available to them more than a decade ago. Had they gone through a strategic assessment, they would not be in their current sorry state.

The property and casualty insurance business and the mortgage banking industry are other notable examples of the risk service companies incur when they fail to do a strategic assessment. Again, with some exceptions, the property and casualty companies did not try to understand their changing economic and competitive environments. Rather than dealing with the peaks and valleys of the underwriting cycle, they took them as a foregone conclusion. As a result, their margins have all but vanished. The failure to perform a strategic assessment led mortgage bankers, especially in the southwest, to misjudge real estate market trends. When real estate prices began to plummet, the bankers were caught with a heavy concentration of mortgage loans.

PERFORMING THE STRATEGIC ASSESSMENT

Although some strategic planners separate the strategic-assessment process into external situation and internal situation analyses, this distinction is not useful when a comparative analysis is required. Separating the external environment from the organization's internal ability to compete in that environment places an artificial distinction on the process. All competitors, after all, compete on the same field. What is important are the comparative dynamics and directions or "game plans" the players use to gain a competitive advantage.

It is far more effective to use the strategic-assessment process to identify the strengths and weaknesses of the service company relative to its competitors. This approach to strategic assessment facilitates the comparability of the data and the subsequent analysis, and it provides a framework for drawing strategic conclusions and testing the chosen strategic direction.

The data gathering and analysis required for a strategic assessment varies by the position the service company or business unit occupies on the client/customer service spectrum. Moreover, the data gathering and analyses are best organized by categories of strategic action. These categories include:

- Markets—clients/customers.
- Human resources.
- Technology/operations/facilities.
- Finance.
- Innovation.

These areas of strategic activity should not be construed to denote the typical functions or departments within a business unit. Instead, they identify the activities an organization must pursue to implement strategy. Such areas must be identified early to provide a framework for competitive analysis and to help management organize the resources needed for implementing a position on the spectrum, a component in the creation of value, or an activity in the service-value chain. An organization implements a marketing strategy and action plan or a human-resource strategy and action plan. These strategies and action plans, in turn, create value for clients or customers. Hence, the logic for organizing the strategic assessment along the same lines that companies implement strategy and, ultimately, compete.

Markets—Clients/Customers

Service companies are—or should be—market-driven as the client/customer service spectrum (Exhibit 2–2) shows. In performing a strategic assessment of a service company, therefore, it is appropriate to begin with a market analysis. As in all five areas of corporate activity, the data gathering and analysis vary considerably according to where the business unit is and where it wants to be on the spectrum.

The collection and analysis of market data has less of an effect on the strategic conclusions and the confirmation of an existing or new strategic direction for a service company at the left of the spectrum than for a service company on the right.

This is because in pure service businesses on the left of the spectrum—including, for example, major international management consulting, accounting, law, executive recruiting, investment banking, advertising, and public relations firms— the interaction between the individual provider of the service and the client is paramount. The ability of these firms to compete successfully rests largely with the service providers. The markets in which these pure service firms operate are highly fragmented and characterized by multiple competitors. Absolute size has little impact on the competitive position of these firms. More important are image and reputation for quality.

That is not to say that gathering market data and performing market and marketing analyses can be dispensed with altogether. Some data gathering and analysis is important in establishing preliminary marketing and human resource strategies for pure service firms. The most relevant data concerns the relative size of competitors and the groupings of competitors according to their relative size. This information helps establish and/or enhance a better image and reputation, which, in turn, helps the pure service firm attract better professionals. Grouping competitors according to their relative size provides a basis for pricing and allows the service firm to understand the barriers for entry into these groups.

The differences in size among professional firms on the left of the spectrum tend to be small and do not significantly affect their ability to price or, generally, compete. The absolute differences, however, between the dominant firms—what used to be called the "Big Eight" CPA firms, for instance—and the second- and third-tier firms in each profession are enormous. These differences often give the larger firms an intrinsic competitive advantage in terms of image and reputation. While second- and third-tier firms may operate effectively under the professional "umbrella" of the larger firms, the success of smaller firms depends more on the relationships between their professionals and clients than on an institutional image.

Assessing the competitiveness of firms at the left of the spectrum is made easier by examining "strategic lookalikes" of the firm or profession. Studying other firms or professions that are at different stages of their respective life cycles can yield predictive value. Investment banking firms, for example, might derive competitive insight on future trends from looking at commercial banks and vice versa. Similarly, law firms could learn much from studying the public accounting profession. About 20 years ago, for instance, public accounting firms began to recognize that to keep control of their corporate clients, they would have to follow these clients around the world. If the nation's large law firms had observed this trend a decade ago, they would have globalized along with their clients. Instead, many law firms referred their clients to law firms in other cities in the United States and abroad and ultimately lost them.

In contrast to firms on the left of the client/customer service spectrum, the collection and analysis of market data will have a greater effect on the strategic conclusions and the strategic direction for service companies on the right. As mentioned earlier, the markets of pure service companies on the left are fragmented and competitiveness hinges chiefly on the interaction between the provider and the service user. The markets of service companies on the right, however, where the service approaches the attributes of a "product," are more concentrated. Absolute size, therefore, becomes a more important ingredient of competitive success for these companies, which include, among many others, the nation's largest fast-food companies, large retailers, and distributors.

For purposes of the strategic assessment, absolute size should be defined in terms that have strategic meaning. Absolute size in terms of numbers of employees, customers, or policy owners, for instance, may carry some marketing or promotional weight but has little strategic significance. Absolute size in terms of capital, assets, reserves, profits, number of agents, account executives, or sales representatives, on the other hand, is strategically important because of the potential marketing and investment those resources permit. Service companies that incur underwriting, inventory, or other risks also consider absolute size an important strategic factor when it comes to spreading or hedging those risks.

Other comparative statistics that are important in the strategic assessment and in establishing a strategic direction are: relative profitability; relative profitability per professional; and productivity per professional. These measures of performance are meaningful in examining a service company's competitive position because of their perceived importance in attracting clients or customers and professionals.

Whether a strategic assessment is for a business unit on the right, middle, or left of the spectrum, the data gathering and analysis should be conducted in a way that facilitates the strategic conclusion, which is described in the next chapter. Whenever possible, the data should compare the business unit with competitors so that conclusions may be drawn about trends in growth, size, profitability, and other variables relevant to the market. Internal, historical analyses of companies or business units do not help formulate the kinds of conclusions that will either confirm or change a contemplated strategic direction.

Human Resources

In the final analysis, service companies and their business units compete primarily through their people, through human-resource policies that attract and keep the best available talent, and through organizational structures that motivate employees and encourage teamwork and communication. The extent to which people matter to any service company is evident from looking again at the client/customer service spectrum (Exhibit 2–2). Again, the role of human resources in the strategic-assessment process varies across the spectrum.

The need for highly talented, skilled people is greatest at the left of the client/customer service spectrum. Physicians, lawyers, and other professionals compete largely on their talents. Another group of professionals—accountants, management consultants, and investment bankers, for instance—tend to practice in groups. They, therefore, compete not only on their individual capabilities but on their ability to attract, develop, and retain other top-notch professionals.

Information about each individual professional at the left of the spectrum is critical to the strategic assessment. This information allows management to draw precise conclusions about the service firm's or business unit's competitive direction. The corporate finance divisions of investment banking firms, for example, compete primarily through a few, highly visible professionals. Identifying those professionals and assessing the competitive positions of various corporate finance units based on the specific abilities of those professionals is critical to the strategic assessment.

At the spectrum's far right, where the interaction between the provider of the service, the customer, and the provider's credentials are less critical to competitive success, information about the individual service provider is not necessary to the strategic assessment. Of course, it is important that service providers at the right of the spectrum—the bank tellers, waiters, package-express drivers, gasoline-station attendants, for example—be trained well and highly motivated. These factors will make a substantial difference in the business unit's ability to compete.

If information about the individual service provider is unimportant to the strategic assessment, comparative information about personnel policies, including incentive systems; training programs and facilities; and employee morale is critical. In retail, for example, Nordstrom's human resource policies can offer competitors a clue about the large West Cost retailer's future direction. Information that competitors would find useful include Nordstrom's policy of promoting from within the company and its policy of entrusting new store launches to employees who have been schooled in Nordstrom's way of doing business. Regarding employee morale at Nordstrom, the following anecdote is indicative. A Nordstrom employee interviewed during the last December holiday rush said that his former employer, another large department store chain, often talked about customer service. The reality, he said, is that his former employer had little regard for its employees, while Nordstrom treats its employees extremely well, recognizing that satisfied employees serve customers more effectively.

Despite the importance of assessing relative human-resource capabilities, the players on each competing "team," many service managers disregard the process. Many managers tend to treat the collection and analysis of human resource data as too difficult, time-consuming, or just subjective. This need not be the case. Often, the home office does not have access to information about the human-resource capabilities of competitors. But, this lack of access is easily remedied by collecting information from the field. Generally, field organizations have considerable access to human resource information—both quantitative and qualitative—on their competitors.

Technology/Operations/Facilities

Although an important component of the strategic assessment of service companies across the spectrum, technology/operations/facilities are especially important on the right of the spectrum. For many companies and business units on the right of the spectrum, the process is almost synonymous with the service. The business units of insurance companies, banks, and other financial service institutions on the right of the spectrum rely heavily on technology/operations/facilities to process customer transactions efficiently. Some organizations even seek to compete through their computer, branch, and agency networks. These organizations often try to achieve service/product differentiation through the application of technology. Computer and communications costs often account for as much as 30 percent of a financial service company's noninterest expense.

Assessing the relative position of competitors in terms of technology/operations/facilities, therefore, can yield fruitful insights about their strategic directions. Many of the changes underway in the financial service industry, for example, focus on the efficiency and effectiveness of their distribution channels as well as on the convenience and possible economies through which future product-like services can be "networked" and delivered to customers. Among other things, an assessment of the technology/operations/facilities strategies of major competitors will reveal the extent to which those competitors "keep up" with and deploy their technology.

In assessing the technology/operations/facilities of competitors, it is especially useful to look at the following:

- Traditional "bricks and mortar" locations of branch and field offices.
- Innovative channels of distribution.
- Computers and communication networks and data bases.
- Integration of technology forward to the company's agents, brokers, and customers.
- Facilities managers and specialized service firms.

The strategic assessment should also include an analysis documenting how each competitor's future direction will be helped or hindered by its technology/operations/facilities, especially in terms of service-delivery quality and productivity. For an illustration of this kind of analysis, see the matrix of competitive operational strategies in Exhibit 4–1.

While technology/operations/facilities are an important competitive component of service companies on the right of the client/customer service spectrum, they cannot be disregarded in conducting a strategic assessment of companies or business units on the left. Business units that compete on the left of the spectrum also require extensive research data bases and interoffice communication capabilities. Executive financial counseling firms, for example, require sophisticated financial planning tools; management consulting firms make extensive use of ec-

EXHIBIT 4–1

Matrix Of Competitive Technology/Operations/Facilities Strategies

Planning
Unit: *Individual Life Insurance*

Nature of Opera-tions Com-petitor	*Traditional Bricks & Mortar*	*Innovative Channels of Distribution*	*Computers & Communications Networks & Data Bases*	*Forward Integration of Technology*	*Use of Facilities, Managers, & Service Companies*
"A"	Closing Regional Offices	Experimenting with Direct Mail	Converting to "LifeCom" Package	Purchased Personal Computers and Software for Agents	Universal Life Product Being Processed by a Service Bureau
"B"	Establishing Center and Satellite Concept	Experimenting with Telemarketing	Distributing all Processing to Regional Centers	Installing In-home Demonstrations of Financial Planning	Purchased an Interest in an Annuities Quotation Company
"C"	Expanding Field Force	Marketing Investment Products through Securities Brokers	Separated Communications and Databases to a Subsidiary	Requiring Agents to buy own Personal Computers	Contracting Telecommunica-tions Network for Voice and Data to Third Party
SUBJECT COMPANY	Field Force is a Base of Competition and Growth	Single Company Representation	Converting to Latest In-house Technology	Integrating "Mainframe" Processing with Agent's Personal Computers	Created a Subsidiary to Handle Telecommunica-tions

onomic data bases and advanced financial modeling programs; and legal and accounting firms require access to Securities and Exchange Commission (SEC) reports and legal data bases.

Whether the service firm or business unit competes on the left, middle, or right of the spectrum, it is important in the strategic assessment to determine how successfully competitors bring the "back office" into the "front office." The operations function of most service companies is usually referred to as the "back office." If nothing else, this characterization alone has relegated the operations function to second-class citizen status, which often becomes a self-fulfilling prophecy. As a result, the "back office" or operation centers of banks, brokerage firms, and insurance companies have assumed a factory-like nature, become isolated from the "front office," and developed a life of their own. In many service companies, the absence of integration and communication between the "back" and "front" offices contributes to lower quality and productivity. Quality refers to a low level of service as perceived by the client or customer. Productivity refers to a cost-ineffective operating environment.

The strategic assessment must recognize that some service companies, to improve their quality and productivity, develop strategies for integrating their "front office" or field force with their operations. Among other things, they install minicomputers and microcomputers in the field, often under the direct control of persons who use the systems, to move their operations as close as possible to the agents, brokers, representatives, and customers. These strategies are consistent with the economic trends in technology and with the greater decentralization underway throughout American industry.

Understanding the technology/operation/facilities strategies of existing and potential competitors is critical because of those strategies' implications for customer service and costs. The large investor-owned property and casualty insurance companies, for example, spend hundreds of millions of dollars automating their agency systems to control their agents more closely, thereby reducing distribution costs. Small competitors and companies that want to diversify into casualty insurance should evaluate the effects of large insurance companies' operation plans.

Some other examples of operations strategies that influence a competitor's strategic position are:

- BancOne in Columbus, Ohio created a market by providing brokerage firms like Merrill Lynch with systems to support new services like the Cash Management Account (CMA).
- National Bank of Detroit became a leader in corporate cash management through its sophisticated computer and communications system.
- The major airlines and rental-car companies compete through their reservation systems.
- Brokerage firms have made enormous investments in computers and communications to keep their account executives and customers.

- Federated Investors, Inc. in Pittsburgh has successfully used technology to directly market its mutual funds and to more effectively process the trust department's transactions of its customers.

As many service companies become more capital intensive and have to compete through the allocation of and return on scarce capital, their ability to compete will hinge increasingly on technology/operations/facilities. A strategic assessment of competitors' strengths and weaknesses in these areas reveals much about any future competitive advantage that the company or business unit might gain from the effective and efficient use of technology/operations/facilities.

Finance

Of all the information that must be gathered during the strategic-assessment process, comparative financial information at the business-unit level is potentially the hardest and least reliable. Meaningful public financial information on business units is scarce. Even when relevant information is disclosed, it is generally so inconsistent that comparability is impossible. The same divisions at two different banks, for example, might disclose their returns on assets, but calculate returns differently. Similarly, different insurance companies tend to record their variable life "products" differently, often according to the statutory accounting conventions of the states in which the companies sell their "products."

These difficulties are a challenge rather than a deterrent. They can be partially overcome by not taking the data at face value, by digging into and closely examining different sets of data. Since economic and financial performance is, in the long run, the chief measure of corporate success, it is important to attempt an analysis of comparative financial performance at the business-unit level. Sources of economic and financial results at this level include:

- Industry and trade association data such as *Best's Insurance Reports, Sheshunoff Bank Reports, Moody's,* and *Standard & Poor's.*

- Research reports prepared by investment banking firms.
- Research firms such as the Gartner Group, Input, and Find SVP.
- Government data from the Federal Reserve, the Securities and Exchange Commission, and the various exchanges.
- Department of Labor studies.
- Data bases such as Compustat, Best's, etc.
- *Competitive Intelligence: How to Get it—How to Use It.*[1]

If analyzed and compared at a specific time, the data generated by these sources will not provide much insight into the underlying strategies of competitors. Analyzed and compared over time, however, it will yield those insights. That is because, even if companies and business units follow different accounting and disclosure policies, they are usually consistent over time, so it is easier in the long haul to glean relative trends in growth, margins, profits, and other variables.

Lest managers conducting a strategic financial assessment despair over the prospects of reliably analyzing competitive performance, it is somewhat reassuring that those performance measures most subject to different accounting treatments—return on equity (ROE) and return on assets (ROA), for example—may not necessarily lead to maximizing return for shareowners, which is the ultimate rationale for the existence of service companies (policyowner value for mutual companies).[2] Instead, shareholder value correlates most directly with above-average industry performance in compounded annual growth in revenue and average net margins. For a detailed discussion of the correlation between the economic and financial performance of a sample of *The Fortune Service 500* companies and shareholder value, see the Appendix and Chapter 8.

The strategic financial and economic assessment will generate conclusions about the underlying reasons for the varia-

---

[1]Leonard M. Fuld, *Competitor Intelligence: How to Get It, How to Use It* (New York: John Wiley & Sons, 1985).

[2]Alfred Rappaport, *Creating Shareowner Value: A New Standard for Business Performance* (New York: Free Press, 1986).

tions in performance among business units. These reasons relate to pricing policies, reserving policies, sales-force productivity, overhead costs, distribution costs, and the possible depth and breadth of services.

Innovation

The final component of the strategic-assessment process is innovation. Creativity and resourcefulness—innovativeness—is the lifeblood of successful service enterprises. No competitive strategic assessment can, therefore, be complete without a thorough and rigorous examination of how one's own company or business unit compares on this score.

In assessing the innovativeness of competitors, there is no substitute for examining their track records for new services, new products, new strategies, and research and development. Since innovation is baked into the fabric, since it is integral to the corporate culture of some service companies, history is usually a good indicator of future innovative behavior. In financial services, for example, Citicorp has consistently led in the introduction and development of consumer financial services. Through consistently upgraded Automated Teller Machines, the Citicard, Direct Access, Citicorp Travelers Checks, and the CitiOne statement, Citicorp has fueled growth, improved margins, erected large competitive barriers, and revolutionized consumer banking.

Again, in financial services, Merrill Lynch secured a "first mover" and, finally, a lasting competitive advantage through its Cash Management Account (CMA). More than a decade has passed since the introduction of the CMA, and Merrill Lynch still has about a 60 percent share of the market for all cash-management accounts in the United States. Any company that wants to compete with Merrill Lynch on the retail front has to deal with this competitive reality.

In retail, it suffices only to look at Nordstrom, the large West Coast department-store chain, which, unlike many competitors, has been innovative, especially in its human-resource strategies. Wal-Mart is consistently innovative in identifying new markets, serving them with hyperstores, and merchandising effectively. In the package-express business, Federal Express is innovative in its technology/operations strategy and in recognizing the need for a strong network to bind all major cities in the United States. In the entertainment industry, Disney has innovatively improved on its original franchise. National Car Rental has distinguished itself from competitors through higher quality of service, better productivity, and innovative provisional schemes.

When it leads to a "first mover" advantage, innovation helps service companies secure a lasting competitive advantage. In some cases—Federal Express, National Car Rental, McDonald's, Toys "Я" Us, Disney, and Wal-Mart, for example—innovation has translated into industry leadership. In all cases, innovative companies went through a strategic-assessment process. Note that except for Federal Express, which is a relatively young company, the other service companies discussed here are mature, and Toys "Я" Us, in fact, rose from the ashes of the bankrupt Interstate Stores. What this means is that in examining innovation in the strategic-assessment process, it is important to look closely not only at start-up or young competitors but at mature and reemerging competitors.

The innovation component of the strategic assessment might be viewed as yielding preliminary answers to the question "What must we do to achieve a lasting competitive advantage?" This question, in turn, translates into more specific questions, including:

- What changes are likely to occur in demographics and consumer behavior or market needs?
- How is our competition likely to respond to these potential market changes?
- Is our competition likely to respond to these potential market changes?
- Can our service company benefit from competitors' early moves and become a "fast follower?"

The overall strategic-assessment process, which is depicted in the flow chart on page 66, provides an analytical framework for using the tools in Chapter 2: the service life cycle; the client/customer service spectrum; the creation of service value;

and the service-value chain. Together, the framework and the tools are critical in assessing the relative competitive position of a service company or business unit in each market the company or unit chooses to serve.

When conducted carefully and thoroughly, the strategic-assessment process serves as the beginning of strategy implementation in a service company. That is, to be effective, the process requires nearly everyone in the service company or business unit to participate, making any necessary change easier to execute. In forging and executing specific strategies, however, the strategic assessment can only be as effective as the conclusions that are drawn from the assessment.

CHAPTER 5

STRATEGIC CONCLUSIONS AND DIRECTION

Having completed the strategic-assessment process, service managers must then draw strategic conclusions based on the assessment results. The conclusions make it possible for service managers to test the viability of their hypothetical direction. In some instances, the conclusions derived from the assessment will confirm the chosen strategic direction; in other instances, the conclusions will argue for changing the direction or abandoning it altogether.

Developing strategic conclusions may seem so obvious that one might question treating it as an independent, specific activity. But the activity must be treated independently because it is the most ignored step in the process of strategic thinking. Developing sound conclusions is neglected largely because it is such a wrenching process for most organizations, for service and manufacturing companies alike.

Drawing conclusions from the assessment findings forces managers to look hard at themselves and their organization. A frightening prospect for many managers; they must see themselves as others see them. After completing the conclusion phase of the strategic thinking process, the president of a bank said that he felt like pulling down the curtain on the front door and "shutting the place down."

The conclusions phase—like the overall strategic thinking process—is, by nature, self-critical. At best, as an insurance company executive described it, it is "like wearing a hair shirt." At worst, the process is destructive. Just because the process may have negative consequences, however, does not mean that it should not be undertaken. The process must be implemented carefully, sensitively, and with the total involvement of the service company's leadership. Rather than embarking upon this painful process with negative judgments about what is wrong with the organization, the process should be approached with a sense of what needs to be done to succeed. The attitudinal distinction here is important.

DEFINING THE STRATEGIC CONCLUSION

As used in the overall context of the strategic thinking process, strategic conclusion is the activity that helps managers identify what must be done to achieve lasting competitive advantage. It helps managers identify the actions a company must take in overcoming its weaknesses to create value, and what managers must do to serve their chosen markets. The client/customer service spectrum, of course, helps identify the market segment(s) that business-unit managers choose to serve. The creation of service value and the service-value chain—the other strategic tools available to service companies—help managers determine the basis of competition. Exhibit 2–9 illustrates a competitive analysis worksheet which shows *what* a service company—in this case, commercial/investment bank—must do to create lasting competitive advantage. What a service company must do is also shown in terms of the spectrum, the components of service value, the activity chain, and the areas of strategic action.

Strategic conclusions must be based on the facts; observations; qualitative and quantitative analyses; and judgments made during the strategic assessment. The conclusions are not just a careful presentation of the data but logical deductions or inferences made from the data. Strategic conclusions represent the foundation of truth that provides the basis for strategic direction. The conclusions must be right or the ensuing direction will not work. Sometimes, when conclusions are erroneous, they point to a direction that could be even more desirable than the direction sought by managers. Such an outcome, however, is a function of luck rather than the result of careful decision making.

MAKING THE WRONG CONCLUSIONS: WISH-BASED PLANNING

As they move through the data gathering and analytical process, most service managers do a rigorous, credible job. The data is obtainable, the analytical frameworks are largely sound, and the process is intellectually stimulating. Often, however, managers tend to jump from their careful analysis to a strategic direction without conclusions, without stopping to look in the mirror and figure out what the analysis means. Alternately, managers draw conclusions from the analysis, but the conclusions are based on a misreading of the assessment or on preconceived notions. These two tendencies represent leaps of faith that result in "wish-based" planning. The thinking is like this: "The market we're after looks pretty attractive, and we hope we'll succeed in penetrating or maintaining our position in that market." Hard, realistic conclusions specifying *what* will be required for the company or business unit to win, if possible, have not been drawn.

Some examples help illustrate how otherwise successful service companies have utilized the entire assessment process, made leaps of faith to a strategic direction, and failed.

A small, niche-oriented retail bank in the Southwest decided to expand, as the chairperson said, "to capture more market share," by opening new branches throughout the metropolitan market area. The line of reasoning was straightforward: "If we don't expand into new geographical markets, our larger, entrenched competitors will take away our niche."

The bank's managers decided to pursue this strategic direction based on a flawed assessment instead of strategic conclusions. The first error lay in the assumption that if the bank did not expand, it would lose what it had. Yet, the existing branches were growing profitably, costs were in line, and the bank's customers were satisfied. Their assessment yielded no concrete evidence that the bigger retail banks in the market were encroaching on the smaller bank's territory.

The second error resulted from the failure of the bank managers to consider that all good locations in the metropolitan area were taken already. In order for their small bank to penetrate new, apparently attractive territories, they had to acquire locations that were either expensive or inconvenient. The bank's managers decided to acquire both kinds of locations and doubled the number of branches.

The third error the managers made was to create a larger corporate organization and infrastructure to handle the larger branch organization. They hired more people to oversee the branches and installed a computer and communications system with greater capacity. In the process, the managers added substantial fixed costs.

The bank's larger, entrenched competitors fought its intrusions into their markets vigorously with both offensive and defensive thrusts. First, the competitors made sure that existing customers would have no reasons to switch. Secondly, competitors invaded the "home" territories of the smaller-niche player. Both programs worked.

The margins of the niche bank turned metropolitan competitor suffered partly due to the rise in fixed costs and, more importantly, from having to take bad credits to penetrate the new markets. In their quest for volume to cover increases in overhead, managers were under growing pressure to neglect or override the bank's credit policies and systems. The bank was caught up in the "death spiral." It was finally downsized and sold to a large, well-capitalized, out-of-state competitor that wanted a foothold in the Southwest. The bank's original shareholders lost all their equity.

Like most business failures, this one is obvious and predictable—after the fact. The example illustrates wish-based planning at its worst. The bank's managers had a preconceived strategic direction they were determined to pursue without ever testing its viability through a rigorous strategic-assessment and strategic-conclusions process. Had the managers not disregarded the process, they could have prevented the disaster. This example illustrates the role that corporate egos all too often play in the strategic-thinking process. The bank's executives were so carried away by their prior successes that they ignored any information that might diminish their power or cast doubt on their judgment.

A southern life insurance company, Capital Holding, of Louisville, Kentucky, offers another good example of an organization with managers who indulged in wish-based planning, performed an incomplete assessment, and ignored the realities presented by strategic conclusions. Among other things, the life insurance company overlooked demographic structures of the South, information that was readily available. Had the company's managers noted the demographic structure, they would have recognized that the majority of the population lives in small towns or rural communities, which are expensive to serve through traditional agency/representative insurance distribution systems. The company tried unsuccessfully to distribute its "products" through traditional channels in major urban centers, competing directly with every large mutual and stock company in the United States.

To remedy this situation, new management was brought into the company, in this case, the late Thomas C. Simons, a former CIGNA executive vice president. He saw the opportunity that his predecessors missed: tapping into rural markets. The data was always there, but the necessary conclusions were not. Capital Holding went on to develop an innovative and sophisticated direct mail and telemarketing distribution capability, which enabled the company to reach rural markets economically. As a result, the company gained a sustainable competitive advantage and a superior financial performance. Capital Holdings' shareholder value has grown at a rate of 7 percent compounded from 1983 to 1987. Its margins have averaged over 7 percent each year; its revenues have grown over 21 percent compounded; and its net income has grown at an average annual rate of nearly 10 percent per year.

DRAWING CORRECT STRATEGIC CONCLUSIONS

To draw accurate strategic conclusions, it is helpful to think of them as the "what" in the equation of strategy determination. The equation, in turn, might be thought of in terms of simple deductive or inductive logic. An example of deductive strategic logic:

> If a certain set of factors or conditions exists (strategic assessment), *then* the following must be true (strategic conclusion), and *therefore* the strategic direction should be . . .

An example of inductive strategic logic:

> A hypothesis is established. It is followed by data gathering and observations that suggest conditions leading to either success or failure. Conclusions based on the data and observations result in outcomes that confirm or reject the original hypothesis and either support the targeted strategic direction or suggest a new direction.

In this instance, a set of independent facts and observations leads to a set of conclusions that is induced from the data. Most business decisions are, in fact, inductive, that is, managers establish hypotheses and then analyze related data to reach certain decisions.

Translating these logical exercises into strategic conclusions relevant to real situations is a difficult process requiring considerable effort and discipline. The task in the real world is further complicated by the need for the conclusions to be sound enough to help managers establish strategic directions that account for potential competitive responses.

To illustrate how a service company might reach sound conclusions, it is useful to break the process into the same areas of strategic action that were used in the strategic-assessment phase to categorize the competitive data managers collected and analyzed. These areas are: markets and customers (marketing), human resources, technology/operations/facilities, finance, and innovation.

Taking the markets and customers area, for example, the strategic assessment conducted by a large professional-services firm suggested that because of the relationship nature of its business and the large number of small, fragmented competitors, there would be no practical limit on the size of its potential market. Regarding markets and customers, the conclusion managers reached was that, given the relative positions and strategies of competitors, the firm would experience no limits on size and could grow by forging a number of high-quality relationships. This conclusion resulted in a strategic direction designed to move the firm further to the left on the client/customer service spectrum.

Again, in the markets and customers area, a brokerage firm in the Midwest concluded that its retail distribution system required a continuous stream of high-quality investment "products" both to retain account executives and clients and to achieve better profit margins than the competition. The brokerage firm's managers recognized that they could not get enough investment "products" from other firms. They, therefore, concluded that to survive, they would have to develop their internal capability or source of new services. This conclusion led to a strategic direction that called for the firm to develop investment banking and capital markets capabilities.

Finally, a small financial service boutique serving the public pension market concluded that, given the emerging market for pension fund investments in real estate and the boutique's strong relationships in the commercial real estate market, it could serve that market by providing quality real estate investments. This conclusion led the financial service boutique to adopt a strategic direction that called for expanding its relationships with public pension funds to develop an outlet for its real estate investments.

STRATEGIC CONCLUSIONS AND THE CLIENT/CUSTOMER SERVICE SPECTRUM

The management process used in developing strategic conclusions varies according to where the service company is located on the client/customer service spectrum. At the left of the spectrum, where the service is synonymous with the professional providing it, and the interactive component is critical, it is essential to participate in the strategic-conclusion process. As a professional in my firm said during a strategic-conclusion session, "You are really talking about us." Professionals must, therefore, intellectually and emotionally buy into the conclusions. While this kind of consensus is hard to achieve, only by achieving it can the firm secure the commitment necessary to implement its strategic direction. The consensus and broad commitment are not nearly as important to service companies on the right of the client/customer service spectrum, where the service approaches a "product" and the process component is an important basis of competition.

FROM STRATEGIC CONCLUSIONS TO STRATEGIC DIRECTION

The conclusions establish *what* the service company must do to determine a sustainable competitive advantage. More immediately, the conclusions help management confirm, modify, or abandon the hypothetical strategic direction. The direction energizes the company, enabling management to determine *how* it will succeed. With direction, management can determine the company's new position on the life cycle, articulate convincingly what the business can be, and reaffirm the corporate mission. The strategic direction not only describes the organization's potential in its new position on the life cycle, but it reaffirms or modifies each business unit's position on the client/customer service spectrum. The direction, in other words, provides the direct focus necessary to compete successfully. The direction becomes the driving force for change within the organization.

A word of warning. Since the process of establishing a strategic direction is exciting, holds promise for the future, and often becomes a rallying point for the organization, there is a tendency to abuse the process. For many managers, easily establishing a direction becomes a panacea, a quick fix that encourages them to avoid the real work of implementation. In the enthusiasm over a new direction, the clear thinking that accompanied the strategic assessment and conclusions becomes muddled. Management's inability to cope with reality and focus its direction leads to fits and starts, to temporary initiatives that confuse the people who implement the direction. Strategic direction is a long-term concept. Treating it as if it could be changed monthly or yearly can accelerate the organization's "death spiral."

People's Bank in Bridgeport, Connecticut offers a good example of the competitive power inherent in a carefully established strategic direction. As its name implies, People's Bank is a thrift institution, which was originally a mutual savings bank. At a time when inept management and confused regulation have put the thrift industry in a sorry state, People's has emerged as the dominant retail financial institution in Connecticut. The operative words here are dominant, retail, and financial institution.

With the guidance of president and CEO David Carson, People's recognized in the early 1980s that it and the rest of the industry were headed toward competitive oblivion. Carson and his team concluded that to survive, they needed to reemerge on their life cycle as a different kind of institution. They knew that they could not continue to pursue their old direction as a thrift institution, and that they had to find another direction. Based on their strategic assessment and conclusions, the managers chose a new direction: to become the state's leading retail financial institution. This direction translated into selecting a new position on the client/customer service spectrum, where they would serve the retail market statewide. When management reached that decision, People's was still a small, local mutual savings bank.

Having determined "whom to sell what," management set out to create value for customers at their newly chosen point on the spectrum. People's choice of direction, coupled with rigorous implementation, benefited the bank.

Interestingly, other thrift institutions, faced with the pressures of deregulation, sought increased earnings through high-risk real estate development ventures and funded themselves largely by direct marketing high-yield, volatile certificates of deposit. This strategy only expedited the industry's demise.

STRATEGIC DIRECTION AND THE FOUR STRATEGIC TOOLS

In confirming the hypothetical strategic direction or identifying a new one, managers take their first crack at strategy formulation. Having decided on a direction, therefore, managers must simultaneously consider how their company or specific business unit will compete given the chosen direction. At this stage of the overall strategic thinking process, determining how they will compete is a reality check. Some of the strategic tools available to service companies are essential in helping them conduct the reality check. These reality checks are indispensable as the first stage in formulating and executing specific strategies.

EXTERNAL REALITY CHECKS ON THE STRATEGIC DIRECTION

Having confirmed their original position or chosen a new one on the client/customer service spectrum corresponding to their strategic direction, managers can readily see the characteristics of the market or markets they will serve and how to competitively serve them.

Service managers must think seriously about how to create value for the market(s) they choose to serve after they have confirmed their original position on the spectrum or selected a new one. Value creation and the client/customer and supplier components, which played such an important role in confirming an existing direction or selecting a new strategic direction, are essential in the reality check since a strategic direction cannot be established without knowing how customers will be served, how existing competition barriers can be overcome or new barriers erected, and how to utilize the service firm's strengths and correct its weaknesses. Using the creation of service value tool and the components of value creation ensures that the conclusions managers reached, that is, *what* must be done to achieve a sustainable competitive advantage, are built into formulating strategy.

A related but often neglected element in using value creation as a reality check for a chosen strategic direction is the creation or maintenance of competitive barriers. The barriers vary, of course, depending on where the service company or business unit chooses to compete on the spectrum. Toward the left of the spectrum, for example, attracting and retaining talented people is a more appropriate barrier than on the right, where creating near-proprietary processes is critical. Whatever the barrier, reinforcing existing barriers or erecting new ones is a fundamental strategy issue.

People's Bank again offers a good example of these external reality checks. Having established a strategic direction and a new point on the spectrum as a statewide retail bank serving consumers, People's Bank managers then asked how they might create value effectively and erect or keep competitive barriers, given their new direction and competitive position on the client/customer service spectrum. People's managers decided that they could create value for their customers through the interactive component by merging with several institutions throughout the state—not for growth, but—to provide focused, geographical coverage to the markets it serves. At the same time, People's recognized that it could create value and competitive barriers through below-market pricing of its credit-card services. The bank's efficient deposit collecting and operational processes allowed it to price less aggressively than its competitors while benefiting from a profitable customer base.

A final external reality check on the strategic direction the service company or business unit has chosen and on the firm's ability to implement the direction is the preliminary market–customer strategy. The diagram on page 3 illustrates the iterative nature of the strategic direction process. Strategies are ultimately formulated, tested, modified, and refined until a good fit is achieved between effort and result. In the context of this iterative process, the preliminary market–customer strategy helps test the strategic direction and provide a basis for the detailed formulation and implementation of specific strategies. Since strategic management hinges on balancing market needs with the organization's capabilities, the earlier this is tested, the better. The preliminary market/customer strategy issues that managers must address include:

- Served markets.
- Services offered in response to market need.
- Channels of distribution.
- Competitors.

INTERNAL REALITY CHECKS ON THE STRATEGIC DIRECTION

Before finalizing a strategic direction, it is important to understand the detailed, specific activities required for each component of the value-creation process. Recognizing these activities—which constitute the service-value chain—is a critical internal reality test for the strategic direction established by managers. While managers need not think through the specific strategies yet and how to implement them, they must determine the feasibility of performing each activity in the chain.

If, for example, the organization's strategic direction and position on the spectrum call for serving a market segment that requires the organization to invest too heavily in technology or that otherwise stretches the organization's capabilities, then how the competitive advantage is achieved cannot be balanced with what it takes to achieve it. The service company or business unit, therefore, cannot achieve a sustainable competitive advantage because it can neither afford to overcome its weaknesses or build on its strengths.

It is difficult to think of situations where management has passed the tests of sound strategic assessment and rigorous strategic conclusions and then fails the final test of internal-capability assessment prior to finalizing the strategic direction.

Wish-based planning, however, can occur at this stage of the strategic-thinking process. The use of the service-value chain, therefore, to test the feasibility of the chosen direction, is not a frivolous exercise.

If a preliminary market/customer strategy provided a good external reality check on strategic direction, a preliminary human-resource strategy provides an equally effective internal check. The preliminary human resource strategy issues that managers must address include:

- Talent and skills.
- Numbers of people.
- Organizational structures.
- Management style.
- Reward systems.
- Culture and values.

If a service company or business unit has established a strategic direction and targeted a market to serve that is inconsistent with its human-resource strategy and capability—or inconsistent with any other resource required to serve the market—the earlier the inconsistency surfaces the better.

CONFIRMATION OF THE BUSINESS-UNIT ROLE WITHIN THE CORPORATION

Recall what was suggested earlier in Chapter 3—that the careful selection of business units is critical to the process of strategic thinking. A strategic direction and specific strategies are not implemented by planning staffs or even, at least directly, by senior managers. They are implemented by the people who participated most directly in the process, by people who are accountable for execution. Those people reside in the business units.

The appropriate selection of business units, therefore, provides an essential focus on the targeted market and on the organization's internal ability to serve the market. While many factors come into play when managers decide how to structure an enterprise, the selection of business units—particularly market-focused units—underscores the rationale for a particular kind of structure. Regardless of how managers structure their organization, however, the selection of business units is important both as a vehicle for market-focused strategies and as an engine for implementation.

The importance of the business unit as the real focus of strategy and implementation does not diminish the corporate staff's role as noted in Chapter 2. This role is best illustrated by example. The Greyhound Corporation, under the able leadership of chairman and CEO John W. Teets, has restructured not only the corporation but each operation subsidiary. John Teets has conveyed to his team a guiding vision: "It is management's job to see the business not as it is but as it might be."

Unlike most companies that appear on these pages—Sears, Roebuck & Co., The Prudential, London Life Insurance, and People's Bank—Greyhound is close to being a true conglomerate with multiple focuses, including financial services; consumer products; transportation manufacturing; food services; and travel and leisure services. Through this vision and senior management's insistence that each subsidiary adopt its own clear strategic direction, Greyhound has done two things. It has shed organizations that were at points in their life cycles where they could neither earn their cost of capital nor re-emerge more vital at a different point on their life cycle. The company has also acquired organizations that not only complement and strengthen existing businesses but that are in the early stages of their life cycles.

Greyhound management has created substantial value at the corporate level by helping subsidiaries establish their own distinctive strategic directions by providing each of them with a necessary focus. Rather than merely allocating capital to each subsidiary and expecting a given return, John Teets and his team work closely with the managers of each subsidiary in the selection of markets, product development, management development, technology deployment, and, most importantly, in keeping each business unit focused. This kind of contribution from the corporate level has made the subsidiaries far more effective competitors than they would be otherwise.

In conclusion, strategic direction provides service companies or business units with a needed market focus. Unlike industrial organizations, whose direction, specific strategies, and implementation are more driven by senior management and strategic planners, service organizations derive their strategic momentum from a consensus for and broad participation in change. Strategic direction gives service organizations the energy and commitment needed to execute change smoothly and compete effectively.

PART III

"WHERE ARE WE GOING?"

OVERVIEW OF THE SECTION

This section may also be entitled "A Strategic Direction." Part II—"Where Are We?"—finished with a chapter entitled "Strategic Conclusions and Confirming the Strategic Direction," which set the foundation for the chapters of this section, the establishment of strategic action.

The process of this work continues with the logic established in the preceding section using the five categories of strategic action as described in Chapters 6 and 7 in this section.

Again, the process of strategic management or strategic thinking is all about the trip and not the destination. The sailing versus driving analogy comes into play. Sailing is a participative sport where the players share a role in the evolving outcome—much as the process of strategic management is an activity in which the line managers must share a role in the evolving direction—*if* the direction is to be implemented.

Chapter 8, Measuring Superior Performance: Results, is strategically placed to connote that the quantitative, financial outcomes achieved by any competitor are just that, an outcome or result. Since strategy formulation is a continuous, iterative process, the outcomes can be tested in a "what if" sense with varying strategic alternatives. The key is that outcomes vary with the strategy; they do not or should not drive the strategy.

PART III
"Where Are We Going?"

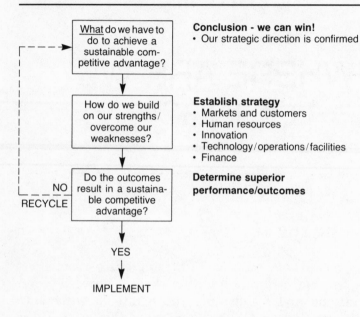

Conclusion - we can win!
• Our strategic direction is confirmed

Establish strategy
• Markets and customers
• Human resources
• Innovation
• Technology / operations / facilities
• Finance

**Determine superior
performance/outcomes**

CHAPTER 6

ACHIEVING SUSTAINABLE COMPETITIVE ADVANTAGE: MARKETS/CUSTOMERS; HUMAN RESOURCES; INNOVATION

With a strategic direction in place, service managers are ready for the next phase of the strategic-thinking process: the formulation of specific strategies for business units. The formulation of strategies is not a fixed, precise process. There is no way to follow the strategic direction merely by translating the strategic conclusions into specific strategies. The formulation of strategies, which allows managers to realize their chosen direction, is based on the conclusions derived from the strategic assessment. The process is really a trial and error, "cut-and-fit" process. This chapter does not, therefore, provide a logical, step-by-step, cookbook approach to strategy formulation, which is impossible. Instead, this chapter offers certain notions and activities that can serve as a framework for approaching the formulation of strategy.

The formulation of strategy must continue to address the critical issue that emerges from strategic assessment, the conclusion, and confirmation of the original or a new strategic direction. That issue is the need to match the targeted market's requirements with the organization's capabilities and the organization's capacity for achieving a sustained competitive advantage in the process.

The definition of sustained competitive advantage varies by industry. Generically, however, sustained competitive advantage refers to the long-run ability to affect a market in ways that competitors cannot readily duplicate. The Appendix to this book, as described in Chapter 4, suggests a quantitative approach to thinking about sustainable competitive advantage. My colleagues and I developed a Competitive Performance Index (CPI), which tracks corporate financial performance with increases in shareowner value—a measure of *economic* performance.

Almost without exception, successful service companies or business units combine a profound understanding of themselves and their markets into their specific strategies. To do so effectively and make sure that the formulation and implementation of strategy are treated as a single, continuous process, it is best to segregate the process into five areas of corporate activity used earlier in this book: marketing, human resources, innovation, technology/operations/facilities, and finance. Again, these areas correspond to the ways in which successful companies muster their resources to implement the programs necessary for executing the strategies they have adopted. The first three areas of strategic action—marketing, human resources, and innovation—are driven primarily by people. The other two areas, technology and finance, discussed in the next chapter, are people-intensive but have other "drivers" such as technology and capital.

MARKETING

Every service company claims to be market-driven. In fact, few are market-driven. More often than not, service managers determine what they can offer and then seek a market. They "push" the service and then create the perception that there was a need for the service all along. Successful service companies, on the other hand, ask, "What do our clients or customers want, and how can we provide it?"

Just as important, successful service companies recognize that they serve clients or customers, not markets. Although this may seem like a fine linguistic distinction, it is not. Technically, groups of customers or clients constitute markets or market segments. But, the most successful service companies our firm surveyed worldwide refer directly to their clients or customers, to the individuals and institutions they serve rather than to some amorphous, depersonalized market.

Any marketing strategies that service managers adopt must be rooted in a clear understanding of their clients or customers. The strategies must also further the strategic direction managers have embarked on at the point(s) of the client/customer service spectrum where they choose to compete. To facilitate the formulation and implementation of specific marketing strategies, managers must address each of the following issues.

Empathy

Achieving a lasting competitive advantage through marketing strategies hinges in part on empathy—a sincere, amply demonstrated regard for other people. Empathy is often confused with sympathy, but the two notions are quite different. Whereas sympathy implies an emotional involvement, empathy calls for emotional objectivity, for the ability to stand back, listen carefully, and understand other human beings.

An example of empathy occurred during a visit to Federated Investors, Inc. in Pittsburgh. Federated Investors, Inc., the largest and financially successful mutual fund, manager, and processor for the trust departments of commercial banks, also is a competitive telemarketing organization. The telemarketing service activity is organized into teams focused on particular market segments. Exhibit 6–1 is reproduced from a large poster on the wall of one of the teams. Empathy cannot be described better!

Empathy is especially relevant to service companies. The teamwork and internal commitment necessary to formulate and implement strategies in service companies are best achieved when people within the company can put themselves in each other's shoes. Moreover, creating true and lasting value for clients and customers hinges on the kind of understanding of their needs and expectations that empathy alone can ensure. Whereas unsuccessful service companies "flog" their "products," successful ones build empathic relationships with their

EXHIBIT 6–1

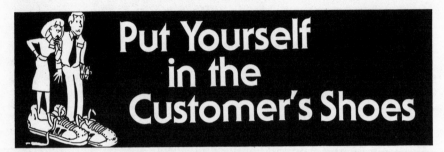

Courtesy of The Dartnell Group, Chicago.

clients and customers as they integrate their customer and interactive components in creating value. The successful companies listen, test ideas, solicit responses, and act on their responses. These companies exhibit the necessary caring that makes them want both their colleagues and those they serve to succeed.

While empathy is of more obvious importance in the marketing strategies of service organizations at the left of the client/customer service spectrum, empathy can be just as relevant to organizations on the right. Although fast-food companies such as McDonald's, for example, create value largely through the process component, they also compete through their identification with customers at the store level. An empathic attitude toward fast-food customers is just as important as the effective process for preparing the food.

Empathy has played a large role in the ability of Federal Express and United Parcel Service to secure dominant market positions. Both companies treat their customers exceedingly well. Federal Express, which is emerging into a mature and very successful entrepreneurial company, has created a team of empathic, "bright-eyed" deliverers of service from scratch. UPS, which after assessing its relative position on its life cycle has reemerged as an innovative, hard-charging competitor, has successfully rekindled that empathic spark among an older, employee-owner work force.

Other service companies that have consistently exhibited empathy as a critical element of their marketing strategies include: Neiman Marcus and Nordstrom's in retail; American Express in financial services; Scandinavian Airways System in transportation; whose attitudes and vision are now documented in the book *Moments of Truth*;[1] and London Life Insurance Company, one of the Trilon Group of companies headquartered in Toronto.

Client/Customer Focus

If empathy is the driving attitude required for winning marketing strategies, the target of that empathy must always be the client or customer. Much has been written about being "close to the customer," but this precept is meaningless unless it is premised on listening to and understanding the customer, on treating the customer as an individual rather than as an impersonal number of a generic category such as "market." The client or customer at any point on the spectrum is a human being. This is obvious but frequently ignored. Whether the human being is a cancer patient at a health-care facility at one end of the spectrum or the recipient of an income-tax preparation service at the other end of the spectrum, the client has a different set of needs with every opportunity a service company has to serve her or him.

The almost infinite variability of a client's or customer's potential need underscores the importance of a client/customer focus for service companies. The focus affects the marketing strategies and, more generally, service quality, productivity, and profitability. To use a quote from my earlier book, *The Quality-Productivity Connection:*[2]

> ". . . an almost infinite variability can exist in delivered services. That is, it could conceivably be possible that each customer applies a different perception of every service utilized every

---

[1]Jan Carlson, *Moments of Truth* (Cambridge, Mass.: Ballinger, 1987).

[2]John C. Shaw, *The Quality-Productivity Connection in Service-Sector Management* (New York: Van Nostrand Reinhold, 1978), p. 7.

time the customer and provider come into contact. Thus, the full scope of services could build to a combined total equaling the number of customers multiplied by the number of services offered, then multiplied again by the number of opportunities presented. There also should be recognition that each service transaction is individual and unique because of the personal interaction between the customer and the deliverer."

Hustle

"Hustle" is an often overlooked element of any successful marketing strategy. In a *Harvard Business Review* article, "Hustle as Strategy,"[3] author Amar Bhide provocatively calls hustle a form of competitive behavior. In surveys of successful service companies, hustle always emerges as a crucial ingredient of marketing strategies no matter where on the spectrum the company chooses to compete. Their people are in the field, working their territories, identifying prospective customers, discerning their needs, and tirelessly promoting their services. Their people have a sense of urgency and purpose. The companies characterized by hustle are usually also characterized by entrepreneurship and drive. Clients and customers are attracted to the spirit, the spark that customer-focused teams with hustle project. Among service companies where hustle is integral to their success are Electronic Data Systems (EDS) and Automatic Data Processing (ADP).

Hustle accounted for the enormous success of H. Ross Perot and his team as they launched Electronic Data Systems (EDS). Both in the company's early days and later, before it was sold to General Motors, everyone at EDS did everything. Senior and junior managers alike rolled up their sleeves and called on existing and potential clients. Senior executives even answered the telephones and took compliments or complaints from customers, followed up on the complaints, and took corrective action. The Honorable Frank R. Lautenberg, founder of ADP and

---

[3]Amar Bhide, "Hustle as Strategy," *Harvard Business Review,* 64, September–October 1986, pp. 59–65. Copyright © 1986 by the President and Fellows of Harvard College. All rights reserved.

currently the junior United States Senator from New Jersey, would invariably answer calls at night, making himself available to respond to customer complaints or cultivate new customers. He knew how hard it was to get customers in the first place and that they had to be acquired one at a time and usually from another supplier. Frank Lautenberg's and other ADP professionals' hustle has turned ADP into one of the most successful information systems companies in the country. Neither EDS nor ADP formed committees or task forces to study customers or customer service. Instead, the service professionals have reacted to their customers' needs immediately and directly. No bureaucracy or functional specialists can substitute for the personal sense of responsibility everyone in these companies has displayed in developing business and satisfying customers.

Pricing

Pricing is another frequently neglected or ill-conceived component of a successful marketing strategy in service companies. Clients or customers along the spectrum do not care about their service provider's cost structure, allocation algorithms, or margins. All they care about is the value they derive from the given service. As discussed in Chapter 1, therefore, "price-based costing" makes far more sense for service companies than "cost-based pricing." The opportunity in pricing is in creating value that the customer perceives to be greater than both the norm experienced by the market and the cost required to deliver the incremental value. To be truly competitive, service companies must find ways to deliver the customers' perceived norm of the value they derive from the service at a cost that is lower than the price the market is willing to pay.

Service companies that have market-priced rather than cost-priced their services and successfully used pricing as a major competitive marketing weapon are American Express, Geico, Fireman's Fund, and Allstate. American Express' pricing of its travelers check and credit services has enabled those services to contribute substantially to American Express' above-average returns to shareholders for nearly a decade. In turning Geico and Fireman's Fund around, chairman and CEO

John Byrne has priced their insurance services in ways that permit them to earn above-average margins at prices their customers are willing to pay.

Distribution

Critical to any marketing strategy is finding the most effective and efficient ways of distributing the service to clients and customers. At the left of the spectrum, where the interactive component is essential in creating value, the distribution channel is typically the professional who delivers the service. At the right of the spectrum, where the process component plays a larger role, the channels tend to be more varied and can include, for example, retail banking branches, home electronic-banking terminals, insurance brokers, direct-response advertising, and telemarketing, among others.

Many unsuccessful service companies tend to mix services and channels, thus overloading their channels and confusing clients and customers. This is understandable. Most service companies were organized along specialities with a geographical focus. As service companies have shifted toward more of a market focus, their functional operating structures have remained intact, especially sales, marketing, and other functions that relate directly to customers. Service companies have succumbed to the temptation of marketing more services through traditional channels than the channels can handle or more than customers can accept.

Also, many traditional channels, especially in services where value is created chiefly through the interactive component—insurance agents and account executives at banks, for example—are so expensive that service managers have tried to lower unit costs by employing those channels "more efficiently." Efficiently means increasing the scope and number of services in each channel. The resulting channel overload has not only confused customers and frustrated the individuals delivering the service, but it hurts corporate returns. That's because often the margins of the services delivered through the channel cannot cover the costs of commissions and other sales incentives required to reward the channel.

In many financial service companies, for example, the customer is perceived as the property of the insurance agent, or the account executive at a bank. Any effort to reach the customer through another channel—a direct mail campaign, for example—is perceived as a threat by the agent or account executive and confuses the customer. Moreover, programs requiring representatives of the channel to sell "push"-like services along with "pull"-like services are doomed. Professionals who are used to selling services that really need to be sold are often frustrated in their efforts to work with customers on services that need to be pulled, that is, services that are bought rather than sold. Carrying lower margins as a result of the commissions required, higher advertising and other promotional costs, these services pose a greater risk to the representative or agent. The risk is that the service being pulled may not measure up to the customer's expectations fueled by the promotion. Or, in the case of a life-insurance customer, for example, the service may not result in a satisfactory adjudication of an auto or homeowner insurance claim.

By and large, unsuccessful service companies use multiple, overlapping distribution channels that cannibalize each other and frustrate the professionals delivering the service while jeopardizing the trust of customers. Successful service companies, on the other hand, limit their distribution to one or two channels per market segment and do not usually mix channels between and among business units.

Competition

Competition is the last component of any successful marketing strategy. Competition gives any service organization its muscle tone. Service companies that do not have fierce competition are like people who, neglecting to exercise, become lethargic. Companies that have been protected from competition are defenseless when the protective blanket is removed, It is no accident that industries emerging from regulation often experience decreases in earnings and average or below average returns.

In the once heavily regulated financial-service industry, for example, companies that tried to thwart competition, often in the thin disguise of "level playing fields," have suffered extensive damage. The companies, however, that welcomed competition and took advantage of the unlevel playing field—Bankers Trust, BancOne in Ohio, Fleet/Norstar Financial in Rhode Island, and People's Bank in Connecticut, among others—have achieved superior returns.

HUMAN RESOURCES

Successful service companies are characterized not only by winning marketing strategies but by human resource strategies. People are a service company's most valuable—in some instances, the only—resource. That this is obvious makes it no less true. There is no first-rate service company or business unit that is not also characterized by first-rate people. Richard Liddy, president and COO of General America Insurance in St. Louis, Missouri knew intuitively that people are the basis of competition in the services. "Good people build good businesses," he said in a strategy development meeting.

As with marketing strategies, human-resource strategies depend on where the service company or business unit chooses to compete on the client/customer service spectrum. The talents, skills, attitudes, and behavior of the organization's human resources must be precisely tuned to the needs and expectations of the clients or customers the organization serves at the given point on the spectrum. Human-resource strategies on the left of the spectrum are based on the self-selection of individuals through their educational backgrounds in medicine, law, accountancy, consulting, or other professions. At the left, firms compete by recruiting, developing, and retaining the best people they can find. Developing these human resources is referred to as education. Toward the right of the spectrum, where the process component is more important than the interactive component, the selection rests largely with the service company itself, and development is referred to as "training."

Successful service companies recognize the difference between talent and skill. The attributes the service company managers invariably mention when pressed to define "good people" are brains, motivation, energy, drive, and enthusiasm (i.e., attributes that add up to what is characterized as talent). Talent is something one is born with. It does not depend on family or educational background or on specific sets of skills. With talent, the individual can be educated or trained to develop skills to the point where talent and potential are maximized. If the talent is there, the skills can be acquired; if it is not, there is little any organization can do to convey the necessary skills.

Several service companies have excelled at recruiting talent as well as in nurturing and developing it. To name just a few:

• The Fleming Companies in Oklahoma, one of the world's leading distributors of wholesale groceries and general merchandise, has created a culture in which talent can flourish. The Fleming organizational chart (Exhibit 6–2) says it all. Consumers and associates are shown at the top of the chart, and the owners are at the bottom. More importantly from a human-resource standpoint, Fleming's employees are referred to as "associates." In response to our questions about this terminology, former Fleming chairman Richard Harris said, "They are my associates. They are our only true assets." What is more, Fleming's staff are not only called associates; they feel and behave like associates.

• Citicorp's former chairman Walter Wriston recognized that in an increasingly competitive, global financial service environment, his institution would gain an edge primarily through its people. He and the institution, therefore, lavished enormous time and money in recruiting talent and developing that talent to its fullest. Encouraging the maximization of individual potential through formal training and competition, Citicorp by 1987 was the only U.S. bank remaining in the world's 10 largest banks.

• K mart has consistently paced its national expansion and store development plans to the availability of talent and to its ability to nurture and develop managers from within.

EXHIBIT 6–2

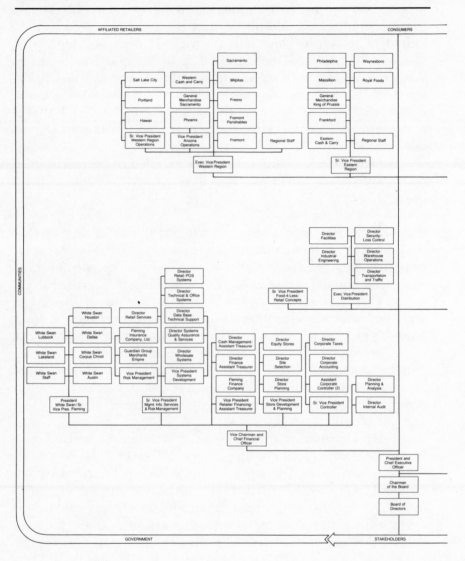

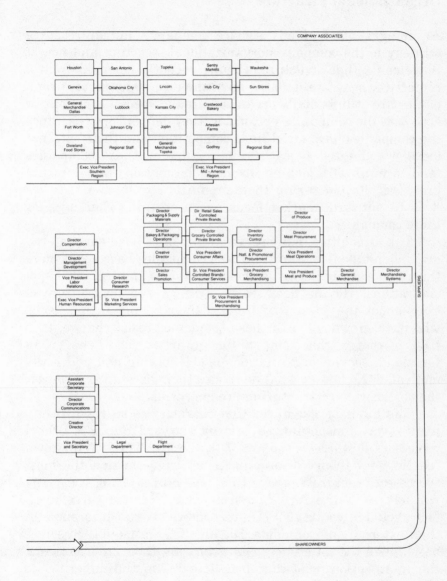

Organizational Structure

An integral part of any service company's human-resource strategy is the company's organizational structure and how it implements that structure. Having recently emerged from a protective, heavily regulated environment, many service companies are still formally organized around special functions or activities the companies perform as they deliver services. Since the companies have faced little competition and their external focus was limited to satisfying regulators, these companies tend to be inward-looking, focusing largely on their internal processes. Restructuring their organizations so that they reflect an outward, market focus has been a big challenge for these companies.

The difficulties many service companies have encountered are understandable. Many of these companies have spent more than a century building up their functional and technical specializations. Having deep-seated feelings and honest convictions about the "best way" to run their business, the people who have grown up with those companies resist change. It is true, of course, that some of the inward-focused behavior in functional service organizations is self-serving and politically motivated. No matter what motivates their resistance, however, the obstacles to restructuring are enormous.

The kinds of structures that characterize successful companies were conceptualized best by Harvard Business School professors P. R. Lawrence and J. W. Lorsch. Their well-known "contingency theory of organizations" suggests that the most successful organizations are those structured along the many variables of their external environments. The structures, in effect, should be contingent on—responsive to—the differences in their external environments. Having differentiated themselves based upon the differences characterizing their environments, the organization must then both streamline and integrate its internal activities in a way that minimizes conflict.

Indeed, service companies that have adapted most effectively to their markets while minimizing the conflict among internal activities required to serve their markets have been more successful than companies that have not shifted from their functional focus. Companies that have aligned their activities specifically with the markets they serve to the point on the spectrum where they compete have found it less difficult to integrate or share services among various business units than companies that try to serve all markets by sharing functional resources. Service companies that align their resources with their specific markets benefit from a greater focus on accountability and responsibility for the efficient and effective delivery of services to customers. A simplified illustration of market-driven business units and shared corporate services appears in Exhibit 2–3. Citicorp is again a good example of a service company that recognized this advantage, and pioneered in the creation of market-focused "mini-banks." Since then, several other money-center banks and other financial-service companies have followed suit, developing their own relatively independent, free-standing business units.

Another aspect of the kinds of organizational structure that characterize successful service companies is the development of customer-service units or teams of multidisciplined professionals who are responsible for serving a particular group of customers. Organizing former functional specialists into market-focused teams has proved a good transitional strategy, in fact, for companies trying to shift from their traditional functional structures. These teams may be organized to handle homogeneous groups of customers based on geographic or other criteria. These teams do away with the need to categorize endless tasks and work steps. They also obviate the need for control mechanisms to ensure that work moves between functions or specialized tasks. They eliminate the costs of those control mechanisms and related supervisory activities. As a rule, the teams display renewed entrepreneurial spirit and enthusiasm, which leads to better customer service and high productivity.

Two successful service companies that have used teams in their efforts to shift from their formerly functional to more market-driven structures are London Life Insurance Company and Blue Cross of California.

• London Life, one of Canada's recognized corporate productivity leaders, has organized its field force geographically into regional offices spread across Canada. The company has also organized its home office administrative support group into client service units (CSUs), each of which is responsible for serving a regional office and its clients. The regional offices constitute the CSUs' internal "customers," while the regional offices' clients constitute the CSUs' external customers. Direct telephone lines were installed between the regional offices and their selected clients directly to the CSUs. The CSUs handle all customer service, claims processing, billings, and collections for their clients.

• Blue Cross of California is the state's leading provider of managed health care to businesses, consumers, and government. Before Leonard D. Schaeffer was appointed president in 1986, Blue Cross of California was a thoroughly functional organization serving all its markets through a network of field offices and processing centers. Schaeffer reorganized the company along client–customer lines into units called market business units (MBUs). The MBUs were given the freedom to organize as they saw fit to meet the distinctive needs of their respective markets. Under Schaeffer's direction, Mark Weinberg, senior vice president of the Individual Services Division, led the consumer MBU, a unit on the far right of the client/customer service spectrum. Mark Weinberg and his team pulled together all customers to be served by the consumer MBU into a separate, totally revamped facility in Westlake, California. Mark Weinberg and his team further organized their customers into Customer Service Units (CSUs) by zip code and provided nearly all the services customers required through the CSUs. The result has been a substantial rise in the quality of service and in productivity.

Despite everything written on management style, including the alphabet theories, for example, and a whole slew of books on Japanese management, the term *management style* is a misnomer. In the service sector, at least, the term *leadership style* should replace management style. The notion of leadership rather than management is consistent with the ideal organizational structure for service companies, that is, one that promotes flatter, mutually cooperative, customer-oriented teams that function fairly autonomously with minimal controls. The leadership style varies, of course, by where the service organization is on the client/customer service spectrum. Organizations at the left—where value is created chiefly through the interactive component and professionals delivering the service—call for a personal leadership style based on consensus and commitment. Talented, highly motivated professionals do not respond to a leadership style that does not take personal values, feelings, opinions, and experience into account.

As one moves across the spectrum toward the right—where value is created largely through the process component and the interaction between the provider and consumer of the service is not as critical—consensus and broad-based commitment are less important. Even here, however, a leadership style characterized by empathy and sensitivity works best. The traditional American hierarchical, top-down management style, where people at lower levels of an organization are told what to do, is obsolete. Like the implementation of market-driven organizational structures, executing a leadership style rather than a management style can be problematic. After all, most managers today grew up deeply influenced by the military and General Motors as role models of management. Nevertheless, successful service companies are gradually dispelling these notions and rejuvenating themselves through an approach to human-resource management that is closer to leadership.

Reward systems are integral to the leadership of service companies. Successful service managers have found that the behavior of their professionals is directly influenced by how they are rewarded. Rewards are not merely salaries, bonuses, or other forms of financial remuneration. Rewards also include all those subtle but critical signals from managers that the "associates" are performing in ways valued by the company. Such rewards may include committee assignments, for instance, special leadership roles in task forces, promotions, or simply an occasional compliment. No matter what form the reward takes, service professionals will respond favorably to the signals and behave accordingly.

INNOVATION

Combined with purposeful, clearly articulated, and client/customer-driven marketing and human-resource strategies, innovation is the lifeblood of the successful service company. Innovation allows the company to get new vitality by repositioning itself on the life cycle. Innovation promotes greater enthusiasm, commitment, and excitement within the organization. Innovation allows service companies to achieve "first-mover" benefits and, through them, lasting competitive advantage.

So much of the business literature and the substance of motivational seminars extols the virtues of innovative thinking; it makes one wonder why all companies are not more innovative. The answer is straightforward: risk and the status quo. The comfort and security of what is known and a fear of the unknown are powerful deterrents against innovation. Without a willingness to change, innovation strategies can be neither formulated nor executed.

Product versus Service

Much of the research and writing on innovation has focused on products and the manufacturing companies that make them. When they are treated at all, services seldom get equal time. Students of innovation do not distinguish between product companies and service companies probably because they do not believe that the distinction is relevant or because there are not enough clear-cut examples of innovation in the service sector from which to draw conclusions.

Yet, there are many examples of service companies that owe their success to innovation strategies. Similarly, there are many companies whose failures can be attributed directly to their inability to think innovatively. What these examples and other research reveals is that innovation differs according to whether one is dealing with a product or a service. Strategies that work for manufacturing companies cannot be readily transferred to service companies. Among the chief differences is the intangibility of the service.

An idea or a concept alone, in the absence of something tangible, is exceedingly difficult to sell both inside and outside an organization. A concept that led to a product was the Post It™ notes at 3M. While it was slow to gain acceptance within 3M and difficult to market test, the product was tangible enough for its potential popularity to be tested with the company's secretarial force.

Just how intangible a service is can be seen in Exhibit 2–3 in Chapter 2. A reexamination of the components of a service through which value is created shows that all the components, at any point on the client/customer service spectrum, are characterized by people. It is the people—their attitudes, expectations, needs, behavior, talents, and skills—who, combined with capital, make up the service "product." Innovation strategies in service companies, therefore, must account for the changes in the ways that people interact with other people. This is true to a much greater degree in service companies than in product-based companies.

Virtually all the well-known service-sector successes in innovation—and many successes in the manufacturing sector as well—have occurred through small groups of highly motivated people working closely together in so-called "skunk works," developing models or prototypes of the new service in pilot projects. Large, seemingly bureaucratic companies have developed new services with pilot projects executing through "skunk works." Entire industries, in fact—the package-express industry, for example—have grown up through pilot projects. When properly communicated, recognized, and rewarded within the company, this kind of innovation has demonstrated to the "doubting Thomases" and the "bush sitters" of the most risk-averse companies that they, too, may be successful innovators.

New services created through pilot projects at large, traditional service companies that demonstrate it can be done include, among others:

- The Discover Card at Sears, Roebuck & Co.
- The Dow Jones Computer Network at Dow Jones.
- The Cash Management Account (CMA) at Merrill Lynch with the support of BancOne's innovative input. The

CMA has been so successful that even though it was launched over a decade ago, it still has about 60 percent of the market.

- Trintext Services, now called Pordigy, a joint venture between Sears and IBM.
- The proliferation of new services and merchant groups through "The Card" at American Express.
- The small-package express business at the United Parcel Service.
- The expansion of services provided by the Sabre System at American Airlines.
- The recovery and surge of momentum at Disney.
- The continued expansion of retail banking at Citicorp.

Whether the innovating company is large or small, most successful innovation occurs through small teams of risk takers operating outside the normal corporate channels. It is far more difficult to effect change and innovate through routine management processes. Few, if any, major innovations result from highly structured planning systems.

Client/Customer Focus

It is important to recognize that service-sector innovation begins with the client or customer. Service concepts or "products" in search of customers are difficult to turn into successes. To work, service innovation requires empathy and listening closely to what clients or customers are saying even when they are clearly articulating their wishes. Few have said this better than James Brian Quinn. In his *Harvard Business Review* article, "Managing Innovation: Controlled Chaos,"[4] Quinn says that the most successful innovation occurs in response to or in anticipation of customer needs or requirements. In the course of many consulting assignments, my partners and I have characterized the innovative response of service companies and in-

---

[4] James Brian Quinn, "Managing Innovation: Controlled Chaos," *Harvard Business Review* 63, no. 3 (May–June 1985), pp. 73–84. Copyright 1985 by the President and Fellows of Harvard College. All rights reserved.

dividuals as "entrepreneurial innovation." In his recent work, *Innovation and Entrepreneurship*,[5] Peter Drucker reverses the order of those words. The connection between them is important regardless of whether they refer to a leadership style or to a process whereby service companies can succeed.

The Interactive and Process Components

Since the interactive component is the link between the client or customer and the process through which the service is delivered, the importance of the component in any innovation strategy is critical. London Life Insurance Company of Toronto, a company cited often in this work, offers a good example of how an organization that has created a culture of innovation has adapted its innovative thinking to the interactive component of its service.

In 1983, London Life began to address a long list of issues dealing with the service it provided its customer market through its "single-company" agent sales force. These issues included:

- Creating a tighter bond between the company's agents (the interactive component), its customers, and its home office (the process component).
- Providing a vehicle for testing and delivering new services to a growing customer base.
- Developing a more productive service-delivery process so that the growing agent force could generate higher sales per agent.

At the same time, London Life wanted to build on its considerable customer and agent loyalty to develop a strategy for achieving a lasting competitive advantage.

London Life's North American competitors had tried to improve the linkage between their companies and customers through various means. These included: bypassing the agent

---

[5]Peter F. Drucker, *Innovation and Entrepreneurship: Practice and Principles,* (Harper and Row, 1985)

through alternative channels of distribution, requiring agents to buy personal computers so that they could demonstrate their financial services to existing and prospective customers, and through direct connections to the home office's mainframe computer and "dumb terminals" in the branch offices. At best, the results were marginal. At worst, these efforts to improve the linkage turned into a costly turnoff for both customers and agents who felt increasingly manipulated for the benefit of the companies.

Instead of pursuing any of these alternatives, London Life created a project its chairman and CEO Earl H. Orser named "Wind Tunnel." As the name implies, "Wind Tunnel" as a "test bed" for issues the company faced in its efforts to achieve competitive advantage. To implement "Wind Tunnel," London Life used both pilot projects and "skunk works." The latter consisted of a project task force staffed by professionals from sales, administration, and information systems led by William Kennedy, a highly regarded staff member with sales-management experience. He, in turn, had active support from top management.

The small team of six to eight closely affiliated players developed and implemented "Wind Tunnel" with the sales organization representing 6 of the more than 100 field offices. The project was designed in response to anticipated customer needs and with enormous field sales counsel and help. It was not a home office project. The entire process of planning, developing, and implementing the concept in the six offices transpired in less than one year for a budgeted amount that was a mere fraction of what other large-scale implementation efforts cost.

The results of the pilot project have been gratifying. Among them:

- An enthusiastic and committed sales force has achieved sales targets well above company averages.
- Customers who, when canvassed in focus groups, have conveyed positive feelings about "Wind Tunnel."
- A team confident in the knowledge that it has made a substantial contribution to the company.

During the last four years, "Wind Tunnel" has been rolled out across Canada. While technically "Wind Tunnel" can be duplicated by London Life's competitors, the real basis of competitive advantage, as London Life managers are well aware, lies in how well customers, agents, and home-office personnel use the tool to provide the necessary network for improving communications and reducing the transaction costs among the various components of the service-delivery process. "Wind Tunnel" or "Gateway," as the fully implemented concept is now called, has also served as a successful model for pursuing other innovative concepts and processes throughout London Life.

Innovation has been highlighted as a discrete area of strategic action in this book so as to not turn innovation into a formal process. Rather, it is highlighted to make sure that service managers pay it respect. There is no successful service company that has not woven innovation into the fabric of its organization.

CHAPTER 7

ACHIEVING SUSTAINABLE COMPETITIVE ADVANTAGE: TECHNOLOGY/OPERATIONS/ FACILITIES AND FINANCE

Unlike the three areas of strategic action discussed in the last chapter, the remaining two areas—technology/operations/facilities (TOF) and finance—are often neglected. Service companies seldom assign TOF and finance the strategic independence and priority they deserve. Yet, the successful formulation and execution of integrated strategies depend increasingly on recognizing their role. The rapidly escalating costs of TOF in many service companies, the uncertainty of benefits derived from TOF investments, and the closer links between TOF and the other strategic-action areas make TOF more strategically important than ever. Like TOF, finance has acquired greater strategic significance. That is largely because of the greater capital intensity of many service companies, the bewildering proliferation of financial instruments, and the growing number and complexity of financial risks that companies incur.

TECHNOLOGY/OPERATIONS/FACILITIES

Many service managers claim to compete through the effectiveness, efficiency, and innovativeness of their TOF strategies. In reality, few do. In the service sector—especially in financial services—huge investments in TOF are seldom perceived as paying off. These investments have neither helped service companies achieve their expected economic returns through lower operating costs nor helped them gain a sustained competitive advantage. Yet, service managers feel compelled to keep investing in TOF for fear that if they do not, their competitors will gain an edge. "We're damned if we do, and we're damned if we don't" says an executive at a money-center bank.

That successful TOF strategies are possible is clear from the few service companies that have used them. Those companies include: American Airlines, American Express, Citicorp, First Wachovia, Merrill Lynch, the National Bank of Detroit, and Sears, Roebuck and Co. Like other service companies that have succeeded in their TOF strategies, these companies recognize what it takes. To compete successfully through TOF strategies, companies or the appropriate business units must create value. To create value, in turn, they must ensure that the cost of TOF activities is less than the prices they can charge and that their customers perceive the value in terms of benefits derived as they serve their customers.

TOF strategies, therefore, succeed when they:

- Match the needs of the customers on any given point along the client/customer service spectrum.
- Create value for the customer at a cost that can be recovered in the price of the service.
- Lower the unit cost per transaction.
- Lock the customer into the service or, to put it another way, when they entail high switching costs permit a high degree of focus by serving niche markets.

Extensive research, consulting, and teaching in this area, along with the invaluable contributions to the field by such professionals as Eric K. Clemons and Steven O. Kimbrough of The Wharton School, suggest several factors that are present in organizations that employ TOF successfully. These factors fall into three categories: the creation of value, the lowering of transaction costs, and the establishment of focused niches.

The Creation of Value

As previously stated, the creation of value has to do with providing services that are critical to the competitive success of clients or customers at a cost that does not exceed the price charged for services. Competitive advantage results directly from the increased margins the service provider earns. Sustained competitive advantage, however, results from linking the service company's TOF activities so closely with the client/customer's requirements that switching costs becomes too high.

Examples of these linkages can be found across the client/customer service spectrum. The Mayo Clinic, for example, at the left of the spectrum, draws people from all over the world into its intricate network of specialists, laboratory facilities, and patient-scheduling processes, and other facilities, including a tunnel between the clinic and a local hotel to protect patients from the inclement weather in Rochester, Minnesota. Through its computer-based In-Circle Program, Neiman Marcus offers good customers specialized shopping services, trips to Neiman Marcus cities, and gifts based on the volume of purchases.

Examples of the linkage are plentiful toward the center of the spectrum, where the process component begins to play a more important role. Merrill Lynch has established this linkage in TOF through its Cash Management Account (CMA), which employs Merrill's technological and operational processes to manage its customers' financial assets while BancOne in Columbus, Ohio, supports the CMA with its credit card and check-clearing facilities. American Hospital Supply Corporation, now part of Baxter, provides state-of-the-art linkages between its customers' order processing and the company's own logistics and distribution processes. The linkage results in lower inventory carrying costs for American Hospital Supply's customers and in better customer service. Such national wholesale food distributors as the Fleming Companies, Super Value, and Sysco have successfully used TOF to link their supermarket customers with the suppliers of products they distribute. In their TOF activities, these companies have altered the competitive landscapes of their respective industries either by promoting consolidation or forcing competitors to invest heavily in TOF just to keep up.

Citicorp's Retail Banking Group, Chase Manhattan's Consumer Banking Division, and American Express are examples of organizations at the right of the spectrum that have used TOF with positive effects. Citicorp's Direct Access System allows the bank to gain access and manage all of its customers' financial assets—thus reducing the customers' transaction costs and making it difficult for customers to switch banks. American Express has employed TOF strategies effectively to compete against Diners Club, bank credit cards, and other, new entrants into the travel and entertainment market.

Lowering Transaction Costs

The transaction costs referred to earlier were from the service company's clients or customers. The transaction costs of the service company are unit costs of output the company incurs in servicing its client/customers. To create lasting competitive advantage, a service company must not only create value through TOF but it must do so at a lower cost than its competitors.

Unsuccessful service organizations tend to view rising costs as an investment required to remain competitive. They view lower margins as a natural consequence of growing competition in stable, saturated markets. Successful service organizations, on the other hand, know their costs—per customer costs and aggregate costs.

A service company achieves a low TOF cost structure when its aggregate costs are considered relative to total factor productivity. All costs of the organization, in other words, are divided by outputs. Since service organizations do not have tangible, measurable outputs, certain market-based surrogates are useful. These include, among others, cost per customer, cost per claim processed, cost per account, or cost per account representative. By accounting for the substantial shifts between labor and capital that occur in most service companies, total factor productivity helps companies determine more effectively how to lower transaction costs.

Establishing Focused Niches

Successful service companies employ TOF strategies that facilitate the creation of focused market niches. Strategies that "ri-
fle shot" underserved market segments while allowing for a
"first-mover" advantage offer service organizations a platform
for innovation and a potentially lasting competitive advantage.
This is the rationale underlying the profitability of many service "boutiques," which manage to sneak in under the "radar
screens" of their larger competitors, identifying specific client/
customer needs, and meeting those needs at attractive
margins.

Large service companies can employ the same strategies if
they focus more closely on their markets and more quickly by
using their TOF to deliver the required services. Among the
companies that have used TOF to keep up with the boutiques
and, in some instances, to beat the boutiques at their own
game, are Fidelity, The Prudential and Prudential Bache,
Goldman Sachs, and Morgan Stanley.

Factors That Do Not Always Lead to
Competitive Advantage

Factors that are necessary for service organizations to stay in
business are not always sufficient to achieve competitive advantage. Less successful service companies often neglect this
distinction, focusing their strategies on these factors alone
with the mistaken assumption that they will yield superior returns and a competitive advantage. These factors include:

- Superior efficiency.
- Investments essential for doing business.
- Short-term advantage.

Strategies based on superior efficiency, on doing something
better than competitors, may result in doing the old service
better in an effort to reduce costs while competitors have either
eliminated the old service entirely or changed the basic
processes substantially. While health-care financial intermediaries, for example, spend millions of dollars developing new
paper- or image-based insurance claims processing systems,

they may find that they have succeeded only in "paving the cow path." Providers may no longer be required to submit claims or they can submit them electronically.

In many instances, TOF investments that are necessary for doing business may not be strategically important. Bank credit cards, for example, automated teller machines, global communications networks, and extensive distribution systems may be a necessary cost of doing business for some service companies, but they are essentially available to all competitors through direct investment or shared networks. Service managers must not view these initiatives as ways of creating distinctive value or cost advantages relative to competitors.

Competitive advantage may not be lasting. Services are easily duplicated and technology is available to any company that can afford it. In forging TOF strategies, therefore, it is important to determine how lasting the results of a given strategy will be and what the real basis for lasting advantage might be. In many cases, the real basis may not be the TOF strategy at all but the human resource or some other strategy.

Beware of All-Purpose Strategies

One important caveat to remember when establishing TOF strategies is that no single, overarching strategy can possibly yield lasting competitive advantage. Single strategies lack the precision and focus necessary to create value at the lowest possible cost. Instead, strategies must vary by where on the client/customer service spectrum the service company or business unit competes and by the markets it serves. At the left of the spectrum, for instance, where the interactive component forms the real basis of competition and TOF is not as critical, strategies will differ from those at the right of the spectrum, where the process component is an essential basis of competition.

TOF Strategies and the Client/Customer Service Spectrum

TOF strategies at the left of the spectrum must be designed to support the interactive component, that is, the professionals who are synonymous with the service. The key ingredients of

TOF strategies are: flexibility, image, and quality. Flexibility is necessary to accommodate the nearly infinite needs of clients at the left. TOF must support the professional in her or his efforts to solve the complex problems of the client. Generalized, inflexible TOF strategies do not work here. The unique problems of the clients of investment banks, law firms, private bankers, risk-management firms, and the like cannot generally be solved at any price by generalized processes. The process component at the left of the spectrum is implemented through TOF strategies that incorporate micro- or minicomputer-based models designed to help professionals solve problems at hand.

As in other strategies designed to compete at the left of the spectrum, image is critical in the TOF strategy. The service provider's facilities, including location, furnishing, and decor, should reinforce the clients' self-image. Quality is as important in TOF strategies as in every other area of strategic action. But quality as perceived by the client is especially important at the left of the spectrum. For better or worse, justified or not, images of quality tend to remain with clients for long periods.

Since the process component is crucial in competing at the right of the spectrum, TOF strategies warrant far more attention here than at the left. The transaction cost is an important factor in effective TOF strategies at the right. As used here, transaction costs have to do with the efficiency and economy with which the buyer and seller of a service do business. The buyer creates value by making the transaction both low cost and easy or convenient to perform.

Whether for fast food, for example, merchandise at convenience stores, low-cost travel, tax-preparation services, automated-banking services, outpatient ambulatory medical treatment, or insurance claims, customers demand both low cost and ease of use. These two factors combine to provide value through the transaction between the buyer and seller. Of course, the TOF strategy that creates value through the transaction may or may not yield a competitive advantage. Whether it does depends on how quickly the service provider implements the strategy to secure a "first-mover" advantage and to what extent the provider creates switching costs.

In any case, to gain sustainable competitive advantage at the transaction level, the strategy must address both low cost and ease of use simultaneously. Whether it be communications, data storage, potatoes, or toys, low cost is most often achieved through economies of purchase. The hard part is combining these economies with ease of use. Ease of use for the customer at the transaction level calls for user-friendliness, convenience, efficiency, and, in some cases, fun. Examples of service companies that have achieved sustainable competitive advantage at the transaction level by combining low cost and ease of use as well as "first-mover" advantages and high switching costs include: Toys "Я" Us, McDonald's, Citicorp, Chase Manhattan's Consumer Banking Group, Merrill Lynch, and Baxter.

Developing Winning Technology Strategies

Without duplicating all the first-rate work that has been done in the last 30 years since technology became an important element of service-sector competition, it is nevertheless important to identify some simplifying factors relevant to technology strategies:

- Application/use/value.
- Technology/equipment/system software.
- Information/data.

Distinguishing among these factors makes it easier to discuss the role of each in developing strategy as well as how the particular factor can be integrated into operations and facilities to forge an overall TOF game plan.

The first factor, application/use/value, is the one that touches the client or customer most directly in satisfying his or her requirements. With a nearly infinite variety of needs, the client/customer in effect determines the nature of the application. The application, therefore, must:

- Be product independent.
- Be flexible and simple.
- Be independent of technological and information factors.

- Permit networking among multiple services, channels and clients/customers.
- Create value and differentiation at the lowest cost of differentiation.

When combined with the skills and talent of people who comprise the interactive component, the application strategy can provide a basis of competition that is difficult to duplicate.

The second factor, technology/equipment/system software, can help the service company achieve low transaction costs through its TOF strategy. To do so, this factor must be:

- Independent of the application and information factors.
- Compatible with industry standards and trends.
- Used to create near-generic, standardized transactions, particularly communications messages.

The hardware component of any overall strategy might be thought of as a catalyst that facilitates the applications and information components without it being integral or, even worse, dependent on these other components. Furthermore, the hardware component is the logical equivalent of a "smart building," that is, one that is wired to accept any type of appliance as long as the connectivity of the appliance conforms to standards.

The information/data factor in the overall technology strategy might be thought of as the raw materials, as it were, which are delivered through the equipment/hardware "conduit" to the application strategy where the information/data is analyzed, interpreted, or otherwise processed into a service the client or customer can use. The information/data can help keep the transaction costs low and the value to clients or customers high by ensuring:

- Flexibility of storage and retrieval.
- Low cost per unit stored.
- Independence from the applications and technology factors.
- Proprietary data bases.

The information/data factor becomes an important corporate resource and a true basis of competition only to the extent that its quality is controlled and access to it is restricted through rigorous security measures.

A TOF strategy is the critical element in the implementation of the service delivery through the customer-focused process component. Depending at where on the client/customer service spectrum the organization chooses to compete, the TOF strategy can call for anything from personal computer-resident software on a client's premises, which is connected through a communications network to a mainframe processor anywhere in the world, to local storefront money stores or individual income-tax preparation offices in department stores. What is essential is a highly focused, precisely tailored solution to each market segment's requirement. To achieve a lasting competitive advantage, service managers must ensure that technology, operations, and facilities be combined to create value, reduce transaction costs, and at the same time, serve focused niches as opportunities arise.

FINANCE

The financial area of strategic action deals with how service companies finance their operations. But as the term is used in this work, finance has to do with more than that. Finance comprises a number of subjects that share an economic underpinning and play a vital role in the strategic quest for sustained competitive advantage. These subjects include:

- Management control.
- Risk management.
- Rates of return.
- Capital allocation.
- Cash flow.

These concepts are a set and, in creating and executing financial strategies, they must be rigorously applied as a set.

Management Control

No one has defined management control better than Professor Robert N. Anthony of the Harvard Business School. "Management control," he wrote, "is the process by which managers assure that resources are obtained and used effectively and efficiently in the accomplishment of the organization's objectives."[1] Process is the operative word here. Management control is the process by which strategies are translated into specific plans and targets, allowing for performance to be gauged against those targets. Management control, with all its links to the elements of management, serves many as an agenda for service managers and as a means of running their businesses. As illustrated in Exhibit 7–1, the management-control process integrates several elements of planning, operations, information, and financial accounting in a way that makes it easier for the organization to implement its plans and strategies.

Management control is often neglected in service companies. Service managers can generally identify with the need for tight operational controls over transactions, but they tend to treat controls over transactions, accounting for them, and timely reports as synonymous with management control. In some service industries—financial services, for example—managers extrapolate bottom-up from transactions, focusing on the accumulation of operational statistics rather than on the long-term consequences of their decisions. Even some successful service companies lack adequate management controls and information. This neglect is in part a legacy from the days of heavier regulation of service industries, when costs and competition were not important competitive factors. The globalization of markets and proliferation of services, however, make management controls now more important than ever.

Two service companies that have successfully implemented management control systems are London Life Insurance Company and the Greyhound Corporation. London Life has "baked" its management control process into the fabric of the organization. London Life's corporate and divisional plans are translated not only into important measures of revenue, costs, and

---

[1]Robert N. Anthony, *Planning and Control Systems: A Framework for Analysis* (Cambridge, Mass.: Harvard School of Business Administration, 1965), p. 17.

EXHIBIT 7–1
Planning And Control Processes In Organizations

Internally oriented processes

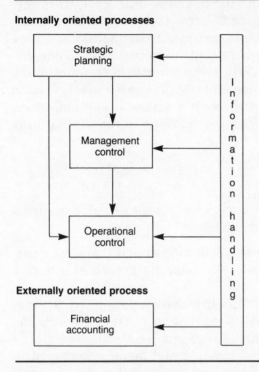

Externally oriented process

Source: Robert N. Anthony, *Planning and Control Systems: A Framework for Analysis* (Cambridge, Mass.: Harvard School of Business Administration, Harvard University, 1965), p. 22.

profitability but also into resource-based indicators of performance such as market share, quality, productivity, and returns to shareholders and policy owners. Members of London Life's operating committee use the information and analyses from the management-control process to highlight variances from plans, to take corrective action when necessary, and to provide a solid empirical basis for the organization's reward system. The management control system has been so successful that executives from all over the world have been visiting London Life to observe the process at work.

The Greyhound Corporation has similarly implemented a state-of-the-art management-control process at the corporate level that serves as an agenda for the quarterly reviews that Chairman John Teets and his staff conduct with the presidents of subsidiary companies. At the business-unit level, the Greyhound Foods Corporation, Dial Corporation, Dobbs House Corporation, and T.M.C., the bus manufacturing subsidiary, have also implemented management control processes, each one distinctive in meeting the specific requirements of the subsidiary. Moreover, these management-control processes are linked to the corporate-level process through a series of key indicators, which were developed through various strategic-planning efforts.

Risk Management

An increasingly essential basis of competition, risk management in service companies involves:

• The analysis of risks associated with existing and new services and with the institution and industry overall at different stages of their life cycles.
• The assignment of accountability and responsibility for risk at different points on the client/customer service spectrum, that is, risk by service, market segment, and business unit.
• The implementation of information and management-control systems that track and help managers monitor the range of risk for each component of a given service and for each activity in the value chain.

Many service companies—notably commercial banks, thrift institutions, consumer-credit companies, and insurance companies—have traditionally defined risk too narrowly to mean credit, or underwriting risk. In today's more volatile, global, and competitive service-sector environment, however, risk includes price risks, market risks, competitive risks, operating-cost risks, regulatory risks, and international risks. Examples of service companies that have neglected the full scope of risk management to their detriment include, among others, Continental Illinois and Baldwin United.

For strategic purposes, risk management is best thought of in terms of the five areas of strategic action: marketing, human

EXHIBIT 7–2
A Risk-Management Framework

Markets and customer risks

- Product (pricing & performance)
- Distribution
- Customer
- Market
- Competition
- Legal/Regulatory

Human resource risk

- Headcount
- Productivity
- Alignment

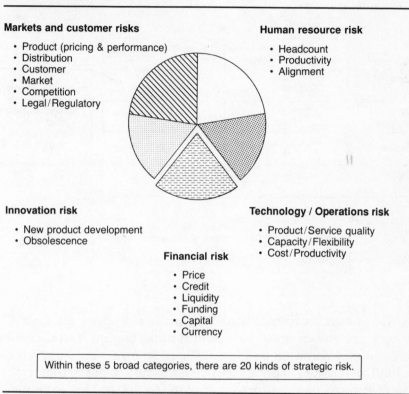

Innovation risk

- New product development
- Obsolescence

Technology / Operations risk

- Product/Service quality
- Capacity/Flexibility
- Cost/Productivity

Financial risk

- Price
- Credit
- Liquidity
- Funding
- Capital
- Currency

> Within these 5 broad categories, there are 20 kinds of strategic risk.

Source: Touche Ross/Braxton Associates.

resources, technology/operations/facilities, finance, and innovation. Exhibit 7–2 elaborates on the kinds and sources of risk that service managers can monitor and plan for as part of the overall management-control process. In all, there are 20 distinct categories of risk that must be accounted for in each core of the risk-assessment matrix (RAM) depicted in Exhibit 7–3.

This risk-assessment matrix takes the example of an investment bank to elaborate on developing a risk-management strategy. The business unit in this case serves institutional clients with straightforward service "products" in the middle of the client/customer service spectrum. The value-added activi-

EXHIBIT 7–3
Risk-Assessment Matrix

Key "product" groups

	Options/ Futures	Commercial paper	U.S. gov't. securities	Eurobonds	Cells of risk evaluation (CORES)
Manufacturing/ Acquiring					• Trading/Inventorying of Eurobonds
Trading/ Inventorying					• Markets/Customers magnitude likelihood timing
Distribution					
Servicing/ Advising					

Key value-added activities

Define the elemental components of business activity:
  "products"
  activities

ties are shown on the vertical axis while a limited number of services are shown on the horizontal axis. The intersections of the rows and columns in the RAM are known as cells of risk evaluation (CORES). Each CORE represents a particular risk area that must be monitored and planned for. In this example, the risks associated with the trading and inventorying of Eurobonds would be assessed along the five areas of strategic action, that is, marketing, human resources, and so on, in terms of:

- The possible range of magnitude of risk.
- The statistical likelihood or probability of risk.
- The likely timing of risk.

The risks, of course, are hedged through various financial instruments and through financial-guarantee insurance.

Several service companies have achieved superior returns and recognition for their strategic management of risk. They include the Investment Banking Group at Manufacturers Hanover Corporation, First National Bank of Chicago, The Prudential, and Prudential Bache. In each of these cases, management understood the nature of the risks and the ranges of cost and profitability associated with the risks. Management also established rules and limits including hedging or reinsurance where appropriate, installed sophisticated and timely mechanisms to monitor all aspects of risk, and assigned individual responsibility for risk management. In every case, management's superior understanding of risks allowed them to minimize potential risks, price their services more effectively, and generate better returns.

Rates of Return

Risk-adjusted rates of return are the basis for measuring competitive performance; for setting incentives and rewards; and, ultimately, for allocating scarce resources, especially capital. Rates of return are inherently flawed as measures of economic performance. They are useful, however, as measures of financial performance, particularly when comparing companies in the same industry or business units within a company.

Successful service companies set rates of return that vary by the service and market segment served. Those companies are as precise in their expected rates of return as they are in selecting the markets they serve and the means through which they create value for their clients and customers. As a rule, successful companies do not use average rates or corporatewide hurdle rates, which combine a "mixed bag" of high-and-low performance businesses and do not account for the differences among business units and market segments or the risks associated with them.

Average hurdle rates, in fact, generally produce below-average results. There are two reasons for this. One is that managers of more-profitable business units have no incentive to exceed the rate, while the managers of less-profitable units assume that their peers will compensate for their shortfalls. Target hurdle rates, therefore, often become the high end of the range. The other reason is that organizations with a high cost of capital have to go so far out on the yield curve to meet the hurdle rate—the often used 15 percent return on equity, for example—that they require prohibitively high reserves, which often reduces their profits.

By contrast, having made up-front decisions about the tradeoffs between risk and return, managers of the more successful service companies make strategic choices about whether and how to generate potential rewards given the potential risks.

Capital Allocation

Successful service companies recognize that there are two kinds of capital allocation. The more familiar one is the allocation of capital to fixed assets or working capital to fund the business. The less familiar one is the implicit allocation of capital to higher risk activities. A failure in these activities, after all, can result in a substantial drain on capital. Cognizant of both kinds of capital allocation, the more successful companies tend to target their returns on higher risk activities—not to the capital they have allocated to activities on their books but to the implicit allocation of capital.

Risk-adjusted rates of return on capital (RAROROC) has been the hallmark of merchant-banking firms since the days of the Rothschilds. Since the partners' capital was at risk, they had to monitor and protect that capital. If they did not, no one else would. With the establishment of government bodies to regulate financial service and other service-sector institutions and protect the public, capital became less strategically allocated. Regulated service companies have either taken inordinate risks with their capital resources or taken no risks at all. Neither approach, of course, is conducive to a lasting competitive advantage.

At least in the financial industry, Bankers Trust has been a pioneer in the effective allocation of scarce capital. When Bankers Trust managers recognized that they could not earn above-average returns on their capital in the mid-1970s, they decided to exit the New York retail banking market. They sold their branches and strategically allocated their capital to investment banking and sectors of commercial banking in which they had strong franchises. Managers simultaneously installed their now well-recognized RAROROC process to ensure the effectiveness of their capital allocation. Since then, Bankers Trust has outperformed most of its financial-service competitors.

Cash Flow

As any entrepreneur knows, "happiness is positive cash flow." Increases in shareholder value correlate strongly with high cash flow. The two observations are related. Cash flow represents true economic reality. It is not affected by accounting rules or other standards. It reflects a company's ability to repay its debts, supply working capital, invest, and pay its shareholders. The financial area of strategic action would not be complete without having set specific targets for cash flow as well as, more broadly, the management-control processes for ensuring that cash flow is targeted as a key strategic initiative.

CONCLUSIONS

Successful service companies find it useful to segregate the strategic-thinking process into these five areas of strategic action. By doing so, the companies find it easier to muster the resources they need to execute their strategies. Treating these areas independently, as we have done here, however, should not be construed to suggest that they are discrete categorical entities. They are not. The five areas are closely interrelated. Although important, therefore, the segregation is a convenience designed to facilitate and lend greater rigor to the strategic-thinking process.

CHAPTER 8

MEASURING SUPERIOR PERFORMANCE: RESULTS

Achieving lasting or sustainable competitive advantage is synonymous with achieving superior performance. Both descriptions of organizational behavior have another similarity—both are outcomes or results of superior strategy and rigorous implementation. Superior performance in today's world of corporate restructuring, leveraged buyouts, hostile takeovers, and international competition for both markets and companies takes on new definition and sense of urgency.

Superior performance is directly linked to superior strategy through the management-control process highlighted in Exhibit 7–1. The formation of strategy includes, as an integral part of the process, the selection of performance measures or what are often termed key-success factors (KSF). That is, what are the indicators that may be used to plan and monitor performance at all levels of the organization to assure managers that they are "pulling the right levers" and that such actions are having the desired impact? In this sense, impact relates to the context of results. For example, measures of performance at the corporate level include such factors as:

- Growth in shareowner value.
- Return on equity.
- Cash flow.

The resulting factors at the planning unit or business unit include economic measures such as:

- Compounded annual growth rate in sales/assets.
- Average net income as a percentage of sales.
- Quality and productivity.
- Employee and supplier satisfaction.
- Community service.

The management-control process, as highlighted in the area of strategic action entitled finance, not only serves as the linkage between planning and implementation or action but as the reward system. Superior performance—results—as monitored and tracked by the management-control process, will only be realized when the indicators and key success factors are directly related to compensation at all levels. The critical measures of growth and profitability are under the direct control of each and every individual in the organization. The degree to which individuals perceive that their compensation is related to attaining the units' results of profitable growth is directly related to the actual achievement of such results. This point refers to accountability and responsibility for results, which emanates from the successful implementation of a management-control process.

An important consideration to reemphasize at this point is the thought that superior performance is a *result* of superior strategy *and* rigorous implementation. Part IV of this book discusses implementation. The positioning of the discussion on results is intended to convey that the measures of performance described above do not, in successful institutions, drive strategy. It is the other way around.

Work with successful and unsuccessful service companies has produced—over time—several key observations that are important regarding how such organizations think about and plan for measuring their performance results.

CAUSE OR EFFECT?

As stated earlier, the number of measures of superior performance are thought of, among the more successful institutions, as the *natural* and *expected* outcomes of *both* doing the right things (superior strategy) and doing things right (rigorous implementation). This is not a "chicken or egg" situation. Earnings or other quantifiable targets do not drive strategy, but they are the results of having identified the organization's position on the life cycle, having identified both the present and prospective positions on the client/customer service spectrum, having decided how value would be created and sustained in a competitive world, having identified the areas of strategic action necessary to create sustainable competitive advantage, and only then deciding if the targeted results will yield superior performance.

Clearly, successful organizations are not "flying blind" through the maze of strategic thinking postulated in this book. Experienced executives understand by intuition, judgment, and wisdom what constitutes "a good business" and set the course for their planning efforts accordingly. "Good businesses" yield superior returns by definition, but superior returns do not always lead to "good businesses."

Organizations "driven by the numbers," call them "financial goals or objectives" if you wish, without the concomitant admonition of "a good business," often achieve superior returns, at high risk, over the short-term. In most instances, the high risks "come home to roost" in the form of bad loans, underwriting mistakes, questionable partners in a network, or operations "glitches" that cause otherwise successful organizations to arrive at or pass the brink of failure. One only needs to look as far as the Penn Square/Continental Illinois or the Baldwin-United single-premium-deferred annuity situations to identify public examples. The nonpublic examples, which have occurred during the course of my consulting work, could fill this book.

Among the key factors observed as contributors to such phenomena as goal-oriented planning are the short-term expectations of the securities analysts and the institutional investors; the promulgation of the process known as "management by objectives" (MBO); and what one of my partners and mentors, Don Curtis, has termed *analog management*.

Analog management[1] is a term Curtis gave to the world of human rules by which many organizations are measured, and indeed, "driven." Curtis contrasts the so-called human accounting rules as a rather inadequate analog for the "real rules-natural laws" of the physical and social sciences. Since we don't seem to be able to measure performance by the "real rules," we tend to use analogs as a substitute. The analogs work well enough, and they are something we agree on, as long as they don't drive or motivate our behavior, and as long as they are used to measure and compare long-term results.

Analog management occurs as a result of the difficulties experienced when we attempt to separate financial or accounting performance from real world or economic performance. The human rules are an attempt to match costs and revenues within specific periods and to place values on inventories. Accounting standards require that in order to cost inventory and match costs and revenues, we set up reserves for everything that cannot be directly offset against revenue, including:

- Taxes.
- Bad debts.
- Depreciation–amortization of property or patents.
- Contingencies for possible future events, including lawsuits.
- Reserves for potential errors in credit or underwriting decisions.

Such reserves, which are often treated differently from one company to another and between industries, not only distort "true" performance in an economic sense, they also make comparisons between organizations and industries difficult if not impossible. These human rules are particularly onerous for service organizations because, due to the absence of a tangible product, only the elements of cost that may be recorded within the system of accounts are recognized.

---

[1] Donald A. Curtis, *Management Rediscovered—How Companies Can Escape the Numbers Trap* (Homewood, Ill.: Dow-Jones Irwin, 1989).

Many service-sector costs are never recorded, including:

- The value of a client/customer base.
- The value of human resources, including the growth in skills, etc., that occurs constantly in a well-managed firm.

While such costs are not recorded in industrial enterprises either, the nature of service-sector organizations is such that the impact of excluding such costs is even more pronounced. This service-sector difference primarily reflects an absence of a physical inventory where the majority of an organization's costs are "booked." Profitability in industrial enterprises, while subject largely to the effect of human accounting rules, is a more reliable barometer of economic performance than profitability figures or returns in the service sector. Returns in the service sector are dramatically swayed on the one hand by various valuations and the exclusion of some of the most important elements of cost—markets and human resources. The final impact of such human rules on both industrial and service enterprises is the low correlation between both shareowner value and accounting/financial measures profitability (see Appendix).

Shareowner Value

Shareowner-value performance, and the difficulties encountered when attempts are made to correlate such performance with returns (profitability), renders objective setting and other uses of accounting/financial profitability data unreliable insofar as strategic measures of results are concerned. Such commonly used measures as: return on assets, return on equity, return on sales, and other indicators that employ accounting/financial determinations of profitability as the numerator, are not always reliable for measuring and rewarding strategic results, particularly in services.

Our attempts to answer these and other related questions have been explored during the course of the author's teaching and consulting experience as well as conducting the research necessary to add a fact-based insightful chapter on the measures of corporate performance to this book. The numerous analyses that were performed appear in the Appendix. In summary, The Fortune Service 500 companies were used as a foundation to test which outcomes or results correlated most directly with increases in the five-year compounded annual-growth rate (CAGR) in the market value of a firm's stock. My colleagues at Braxton Associates and the New York office of Touche Ross undertook the analyses included in the Appendix. From the Fortune 500 companies we removed the following industry groups to eliminate industries that were: extremely capital intensive, still subject to regulation; or for which comparable historical data could not be obtained, including:

- Airlines and other transportation services.
- Utilities and telecommunications.
- Savings institutions.

As the results depicted in the Appendix illustrate, the two independent variables that tracked most closely with the compounded annual growth rate of the stock of publicly held service companies analyzed were:

- The compounded annual growth in sales/assets.
- Average net income as a percentage of sales.

We quickly recognized that while such measures were not necessarily causal; that is, they do not drive increases in shareowner value, they are related in a meaningful way to growth in shareowner value. We combined the variables into a Sustainable Performance Index (SPI) and, when combined with the compounded annual growth rate in market value, we used the two indices to rank the performers in each of the above industry groupings. The rankings and methodology are shown in the Appendix.

The major questions remain. What were the underlying factors which, in some organizations, seemed to link sustained superior performance with shareowner value and what were the factors that seemed to result in other organizations consistently performing at the low levels of their respective industry groups? These questions are raised now to neither praise nor to criticize, but to help in gaining an understanding into the process of strategic thinking for the future. The real issue is, of the many financial/accounting and economic measures and levers that are available as planned results for service-sector managers, which are most likely to increase the market value of a firm's shares?

Among the pervasive reasons for comparatively poor performance among the groupings of diversified service companies and banks and diversified financial companies is the depression in the oil industry. Other reasons for marginal comparative performance in all groups seemed to center around size. That is, it is difficult for large organizations coming off of a large base to grow from a percentage standpoint compared to smaller institutions. Size penalizes some firms, but there are few giants among the Fortune Service 500 companies when compared to all companies in the sample. They are all big and relatively comparable in size. In addition, as shown in Exhibit 1–2, there is little difference between the margins achieved by larger versus smaller firms.

Strategic thinking about results, therefore, must be directed elsewhere for rational explanations of results that will be useful in the future. Factors that underlie the Sustainable Performance Index of sales growth and margins seems to include:

- A focus on served markets—"not all things to all people."
- Relatively lean, flat, cost-effective organizational structures—"a few good people," yielding high margins.
- Consistency—the long view versus an undue focus on quarterly earnings.
- High ratio of variable to fixed costs.
- Innovative use of technology.
- Networking, that is, sourcing of services/"products".
- Leadership versus management.
- High barriers to entry:
     Human capital.
     Relationships.
- Avoidance of growth for growth's sake—recognition that large companies are no more profitable than smaller organizations while, at the same time, recognition that

growth is a prerequisite to organizational vitality, enthusiasm, excitement, and the perception by investors that there is a basis for strong future earnings.

Quality

Successful service institutions, regardless of the service category, from global, diversified financial companies to the community bank, have one common denominator—quality. There is no instance where high financial performance is also characterized by institutions that are perceived as delivering low-quality services. Quality, as a measure of superior performance, is really in the "eyes of the beholder." That is, the true and timeless measures of quality are measures based upon client/customer perceptions. Internal measures of quality have no bearing as true measures of competitive performance if such measures cannot be translated into indicators of external performance as perceived by the client/customer.

Quality is a fundamental basis of competition. This is true of industrial, commodity-type organizations and for service organizations. The difference between industrial and service organizations are problems in measuring and communicating quality against return to the absence or near absence of a tangible "product." The presence of a tangible product, in the case of the industrial organization, greatly enhances the ability to communicate the varying degrees of quality characterized by the product. Whether the product is tested by the Underwriters Laboratory or through a "car of the year award," the physical presence of the product facilitates the "tire kicking" and other observations of quality by the consumer.

Service quality-performance measurements not only must be designed from the perspective of the client/customer, but they must also be "built into" the service-delivery process. Quality measurements must be sufficiently integrated into the major components of the service-delivery process from the customer component through the supplier component. Each component of the service-delivery process must have imbedded within it appropriate measures of quality as perceived by the customer, the service deliverer, or the service supplier. It is only in this way that service quality may be "built into" the service as opposed to being "inspected" into it.

Examples of quality measures that have a client/customer perspective include:

- The time required to process an insurance claim compared to the client's expectations.
- The user-friendliness of a financial institution's account statement.
- Customer service response times, particularly the resolution of billing discrepancies.

Organizations that have achieved superior performance in terms of the market valuation of their stock, earnings per share, or other measures of return to shareholders are invariably characterized as having delivered high-quality service as perceived by the client/customer. There are no exceptions. As the saying goes, "There is no price low enough for poor service."

Productivity

As written in *The Quality/Productivity Connection in Service Sector Management,*[2] organizations, quality, and productivity go hand in hand. They are a set. Indeed, there are no examples of high-quality organizations where quality is perceived by the customer that are low-productivity organizations. Conversely, there are no situations of high productivity characterized by the client/customer as having a low quality. The big question is, "How do you measure productivity in the services sector?" As in the case of quality, productivity measures are also an outcome-result. They are a result of effective and efficient strategies that have been rigorously developed and implemented. Simply because they are the measures of quality and productivity and difficult to measure does not mean that we should not make the attempt and, indeed, successful service

---

[2]John C. Shaw, *The Quality/Productivity Connection in Service Sector Management* (New York: Van Nostrand Reinhold, 1978).

organizations have made significant strides in such measurements.

As usual, our focus is on the client/customer. Measures of productivity by the client/customer may include:

- Profitability by client/customer.
- Capital employed per client/customer.
- Shareholder equity employed by client/customer.

The objective of such productivity measures using the customer as the denominator or as the measure of output are relevant as long as they are tracked as measures of growth. Productivity outcomes may also be measured and tracked by the employee or the professional.

Productivity growth as an outcome of the strategic initiatives of an organization is critical to the continued health and vibrance of an organization as it continually reconfigures itself along its life cycle. Without *real* growth in productivity, there is no basis for lasting competitive advantage.

Employee and Supplier Satisfaction

The words, "quality of work life"—QWL—take on a special meaning in service organizations, as stated in Chapter 7, which deals with human resources. Employee satisfaction, while difficult to measure, may be the most important outcome. All strategic thinking and rigorous implementation may be lost if we cannot keep good people. Therefore, some comparative measures of performance in the area of QWL are important to assure that all areas of strategic action mesh to produce the desired outcomes. Constant polling of employee attitudes and feelings through surveys, focus groups, and open communications are critical to our understanding of "where our people are at." Performance measures such as turnover by experience level and seniority are important to assess how well we are doing and to assess leadership effectiveness.

Not much has been written regarding the role of the supplier in the service equation, however, as stated in Chapter 2, the supplier component is the fourth component in the service-delivery process. Depending on the point selected on the client/

customer service spectrum, the supplier component may take on a critical role. Consider, for example, the role of the health-care provider in the value chain depicted in Exhibit 2–10. The quality of the doctor, hospital, or other service-delivery professional is the basis of competition among managed care and insurance companies. Other examples of supplier importance in the service-delivery process include:

- Retailing and the sourcing of product.
- Financial services and the networking among suppliers who "manufacture" that product.
- Restaurants and the importance of reliable deliveries and fresh product.

Whatever the example, having satisfied suppliers as an outcome of strategic initiatives is a performance issue. Excellent vendor relations at every point along the spectrum not only contributes to the competitive success of the institution, but it has several other benefits. First, by treating suppliers fairly and with respect, we communicate to client/customers and to colleagues about our kind of organization. Second, the more we can "lock-in" high quality suppliers to our firm, the more we can "lock-out" those suppliers from the competition.

Supplier satisfaction, like employee satisfaction, as an indication of superior competitive performance is difficult to measure but critical to assess. Competitively successful organizations maintain frequent and open communications through supplier panels, visits to supplier organizations, collaboration on industry association activities, and through rigorous selection processes designed to attract the best employees.

Community Service

Competitively successful service institutions serve their communities with the same vigor and enthusiasm as they serve their clients/customers. A significant outcome or result of all service-company efforts is quality of the environment or community in which the service business operates. Successful service companies, including the leaders and associates of such enterprises, are characterized by the quality of commitment and the example they provide in community service.

Scope

The attainment of appropriate scope—that is, a scope of services that are tailored to the target market—is to the services sector what market share and scale are to the industrial sector. The impact of size and share on profitability are easy to analyze, communicate, and put in perspective. Scope, however, defies measurement but is, nevertheless, critical as a strategic outcome.

Scope takes many forms, depending upon the position on the client/customer service spectrum that the firm or institution chooses. Scope is an important ingredient in selecting a strategic direction, as discussed in Chapter 3. The realization of targeted scope is also an important indicator of superior competitive performance. Examples of scope help to communicate the concept.

Left Side of the Client/Customer Service Spectrum

Global Scope

Investment-banking firms that hope to acquire or keep their multinational clients require significant origination, distribution, and trading activities in the major world financial markets. Some organizations have achieved such scope through their networks, such as Deutsche Bank, Citibank, and Japanese securities firms; others create value through joint ventures such as Credit Suisse-First Boston; while others are more apt to maintain their global networks through syndication or acquisition. Whichever strategy is selected, if the present or potential service market requires a global presence, superior performance is marked by a global presence.

If professional-services firms, including legal, accounting, management consulting, and executive recruitment, are to serve multinational clients, they must do so through strong, high-quality linkages that provide a local presence. As the saying goes—"think globally, act locally," or in the case of the Music Man—"you gotta know the territory."

Full-Service Scope

A broad range of related services, offered either on a global, regional, or local level are required to serve the sophisticated client's needs on the right side of the spectrum. Whether the professional services categories are legal, investment banking, accounting, consulting, or advertising, a full set of skills are required to serve the varying and ever-changing needs of the firm's clientele. Such skills and related expertise will include: litigation, taxation, actuarial services, corporate finance, research, economics, and information systems. Deep expertise, perhaps including specialization, is a requirement for attaining full-service scope.

Industry Expertise

The services markets are quickly evolving—at the left side of the spectrum—to an industry focus as a basis of competition and as a broad measure of scope. Industry expertise—in the client's industry, is a requirement for credibility: as a means of managing risk—the risk of the service firm—and as a means of focusing the service firm's resources on the targeted market segment.

Industry expertise must not be confused with a narrow, blinders-on approach to client service. However, service firms with too narrow a focus, that is, too specialized, run the risk of "losing the forest for the trees." Overly focused, narrowly specialized professionals may miss new entrants to their markets; competing products from other industries may become such an integral part of the industry that their independent, objective counsel may lose its value; the result is that the client may feel that the service-delivery role can be performed more economically in-house. Captive, in-house consulting services have replaced many formerly independent investment bankers, attorneys, insurance consultants, management consultants, and tax advisors.

Right Side of the Client/Customer Service Spectrum

Geographic Scope

The closer a service organization targets its services to the consumer/customer market segment, the more localized its presence–scope must be. Convenience is a byword in the service-delivery strategy and *economies of scope* is a critical measure of competitive performance. The brand recognition of the following service-delivery institutions makes the point:

- Citibank and American Express as global retail financial-services institutions.
- H&R Block as a national preparer of personal income taxes.
- McDonald's, Burger King, Kentucky Fried Chicken, and others as fast-food outlets.
- Coldwell Banker, Merrill Lynch, and Century 21 as national residential real-estate brokers.
- GE and Sears as home-appliance repair service networks.

The above organizations have achieved enormous visibility and economies of scope due to hundreds and thousands of retail point-of-service outlets. When economies of scope are achieved, they permit some economies of scale in advertising and further economies of scale as a result of refining the process component of the service-delivery process. A few economies of scale are available through bulk purchasing and other shared services. In fact, the economies of scale that exist are often quickly exhausted at the point-of-service level.

Tom Doorley, managing director of Braxton Associates, the Touche Ross subsidiary, has developed a concept termed *threshold scale*. As Exhibit 8–1 depicts, once the residential real-estate firm achieves a certain volume, what Doorley calls the "threshold" level, profits level off and increased volume has little impact on profitability. The same phenomena takes place for most, if not all, point-of-service delivery systems.

Economies of geographic scope are critical to the growth of shareowner value as demonstrated by McDonald's and H&R

EXHIBIT 8–1
Scale Economy Pattern: Multilocation Professional Services Firm

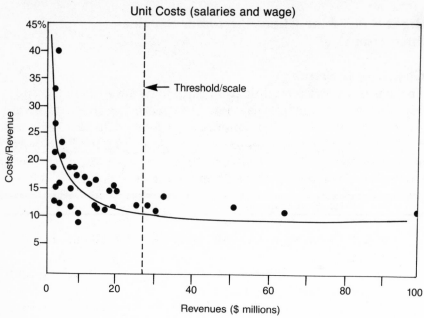

Cost declines rapidly as office size increases, but only for a short period. Beyond the "threshold scale" breakpoint, scale economies no longer come into play.

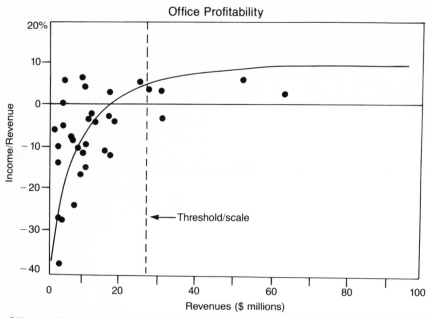

Office profitability demonstrates a similar rapid decline, then plateau relationship at the same "threshold scale" breakpoint.

Source: Braxton Associates.

Block. Neither organization would be where they are today if not for the pervasive geographic presence. However, both organizations realized that size or number of units alone were insufficient for assuring growth in shareowner value. Both realized that their local overhead must be kept low and variable and that their corporate overhead must also be kept to a minimum. Both organizations realized that the real contribution that the corporation could make to local operations was management talent.

Competitively successful service organizations completely understand the distinctions between size, share, and scope, and they develop strategies that are *right* and result in building "good businesses." Appropriate size, share, and scope of services result from having figured out how to serve a particular market.

CONCLUSIONS

In many ways, talking about strategy results after having discussed the strategic-action areas is counterintuitive. It is frustrating for action-oriented leaders to await an outcome. Yet, the power of the idea is found in permitting good people to come to their own conclusions; to let people figure out for themselves how much they can stretch and grow. For the most part, entrepreneurial innovation as a management style will result in outcomes far greater than any "challenges" or targets that management may establish *for* an organization. If people can't or won't establish high personal standards and manage them, what makes us think that those people will manage the challenges and expectations of others?

Part IV

HOW DO WE GET THERE?

OVERVIEW OF THE SECTION

This section might also be entitled "translating strategy into action." While it has been emphasized that implementation and strategy formulation are a single process performed by line managers rather than a multiphased activity performed by planning staffs *for* line managers, implementation is only possible in the "right" environment. This section communicates the characteristics for acquiring or maintaining the "right" environment.

Two major thrusts now account for much of the difficulty associated with change:

1. The formation of a body of knowledge centered around industrial enterprises that focus on specialization to assure the repeatability of product quality at low cost.
2. The transfer of that body of knowledge to service enterprises because there was no other theory available and because managers, educators, consultants and writers did not recognize that a different body of knowledge was called for.

The first thrust made change in the industrial sector difficult; however, the compounded impact of both thrusts made change in the service sector extremely complex to achieve. First, an old, inappropriate body of knowledge or theory must be abandoned, and in its place must be a new body of knowledge currently being written by a new breed of managers, educators, consultants, and writers.

Causing managers to give up the "old" in favor of the "new" is one thing; in the absence of a tried and true new, it is something different. Hence, the uproar over change.

The following chapters provide service-sector managers with some needed help in recognizing that the old body of knowledge was never appropriate for service-sector companies, and that a new body of knowledge and experience is emerging.

PART IV
"How Do We Get There?"

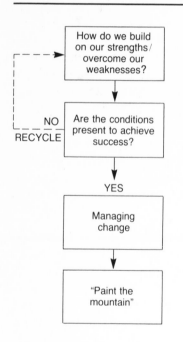

	Develop action plans
How do we build on our strengths/ overcome our weaknesses?	• Markets and customers • Human resources • Technology/operations/facilities • Finance • Innovation
	Diagnose our readiness for change
Are the conditions present to achieve success?	• The five conditions which must be present in order to translate strategy into action
Managing change	**Implement** • Action plans and results
"Paint the mountain"	**Success** • Our visions sustain us

NO RECYCLE

YES

CHAPTER 9

IMPLEMENTATION: THE
ENVIRONMENT FOR CHANGE

Strategic thinking combines *both* superior strategy and rigorous implementation into a continuous, "seamless pipe." Sustainable competitive advantage—superior performance—is all about implementation. In fact, the essence of strategic thinking simultaneously focuses on both the *what* and the *how* of implementing change. This chapter is designed to "tee-up" the issues surrounding the environment that must be present for implementation to occur in a service institution. The "environment" includes:

- An appropriate management style.
- The motivation for change.
- The five conditions that must be present for any organization to transform strategy into action.

In the absence of a fertile environment for change, the tools, technique, and other approaches described in Chapter 11 will have little impact—that is, lasting change and a sustainable competitive advantage will not occur. Indeed, most formal strategic plans are never implemented. A strategic plan that is not implemented is not a strategic plan and is probably no plan at all.

MANAGEMENT STYLE

As stated during the discussion on management style, the issue of management style or leadership is where the management of change—implementation—begins. The term *entrepreneurial innovation* says it all. Entrepreneurial innovation, as a management style, is found on a range of styles about midway between the tight, control-oriented structure often attributed to the old ITT and the loose, academic structure often found in a university. ITT in the 1950s and 1960s was an organization which was tightly controlled through direct reporting relationships between divisional and corporate financial managers.

Entrepreneurial innovation recognizes that:

- People are the "driving force" of the organization (versus even the market, product, technology, etc.).
- The synergistic nature of professionals working together in teams is necessary to deal with a competitive and constantly changing marketplace and environment.

A service enterprise that recognizes, internalizes, and accepts the notion that people are the "driving force" has already traveled a long way down the road of implementation and has established the foundations for managing change as discussed in the next chapter. Organizations that have adopted the management style of entrepreneurial innovation:

- Seek to achieve agreement as to strategy and policy among all of the members (particularly at the left side of the client/customer service spectrum) versus attempts to control their members' actions.
- Foster individual accountability of action while simultaneously encouraging team efforts versus the "Lone Ranger" approach.

The "best" people will be attracted by such leadership. Chairman Robert Winters of The Prudential put the issue this way—"Our staff is our competitive edge; how well we implement a management style and philosophy of leadership to attract and retain the "best and the brightest" will determine the future success of The Prudential.

The approaches or strategies that an organization embraces as the leadership contemplates implementation and the management of change will display subtle differences as one moves from left to right along the spectrum. Certainly the need for more direct control over the interactive and process components is more apparent at the right side than at the left side of the spectrum. However, the management style of entrepreneurial innovation still has at its core the priority of people—their needs, well-being, motivation, and training. Empathy is just as operative a concept at the right side of the spectrum as at the left side.

Examples used elsewhere in this work or organizations that have grown profitably as a direct result of their human-resources strategy and their management's leadership style include:

- The Fleming Companies.
- Nordstrom's.
- Wal-Mart Stores.
- National Bank of Detroit.

Such successes are neither short term in their outcomes, that is, growth and profitability, nor subject to the most recent "management fads." These organizations have established a track record of doing the "right" things and doing them "right."

MOTIVATION FOR CHANGE

An overarching condition for successful implementation is motivation for change. As stated earlier, the organization must be involved in establishing strategy and policy for any hope that change will occur. Consensus must be achieved: consensus is a prerequisite to achieving the necessary changes in attitudes and behavior that provide the motivation for change. The question is *how*? *How* are attitudes and behavior changed through management style and leadership to provide the required motivation for change? *How* is consensus achieved?

Change is a personal phenomena, it affects us as *individuals first* and as members of a *human organization second*. By and large, if a contemplated change benefits us as individuals we are generally in favor of it; if it doesn't impact us favorably or if such change is potentially neutral, we are often unwilling to take on the risk of the unknown, which change invariably introduces. As the saying goes—"Where you stand on an issue depends, in large part, on where you sit."

Change is strongly resisted in the absence of personal benefits. Change is embraced in the absence of personal benefits only when the perceived pain of not changing is greater than the perceived pain of undertaking and facing the unknown.

Having asserted that people change only when it is in their best interests to change does not imply malicious, self-serving, or Machiavellian behavior on the majority of service enterprises. As stated in the next chapter, people resist change for a whole set of legitimate reasons—reasons that must be understood and dealt with. For the purposes of discussing the key issues/conditions for successful implementation of strategy, however, it is important to understand the roles of attitude and behavior on the individual, organizational motivation for change, and how such attitudes and behavior are influenced and modified.

Regardless of the presence of an appropriate management style and the five conditions (see page 168), rigorous implementation does not occur and change cannot be managed in the absence of a major source of dissatisfaction —"the big D." Dissatisfaction with the current situation and the means of coping and capitalizing on such dissatisfaction is what managing change is all about. Dissatisfaction takes many forms:

- A competitive threat to organizational survival and therefore a personal threat to the primary security of its members.
- The immediacy of bankruptcy for whatever reasons.
- A new leader.
- A takeover, or threat of takeover, whether it is "friendly" or "unfriendly."
- A general dissatisfaction within the firm including profitability, growth, etc.

One doesn't have to look back too far to identify numerous examples of organizations that have risen to "fight" as a result of "the big D," some successfully, some unsuccessfully. Among the organizations no longer around, at least under their present names, include:

- W. T. Grant—gone.
- E. J. Korvette—gone.
- E. F. Hutton (now part of Shearson American Express).
- Crocker Bank (now a part of Wells Fargo).
- Peoples Express (now a part of Texas Air).
- Food Fair (now Pantry Pride).
- Best & Co.—gone.
- Penn Square Bank—gone.
- National Bank of North America (now a part of National Westminster Bank).
- Finley Kumble—gone.

Others, motivated strongly by a desire for survival, used "the big D" to turn themselves around, remain independent, and rigorously implemented strategies that now permit some to classify them as "winners":

- A&P.
- Bankers Trust.
- Disney.
- Fireman's Fund.
- GEICO.
- K mart.
- Montgomery Ward.
- Peoples Bank.
- Toys"Я"Us.
- Woolworth.

Others are fighting for their lives, highly motivated by "the big D":

- Bank of America.
- Macys (a leveraged buyout).
- AVIS (a leveraged buyout).
- Federated and Allied Stores (taken over by Campau).

- Eastern and Continental (taken over by Texas Air).
- Safeway (a leveraged buyout).
- Brooks Brothers (acquired by Marks & Spencer).
- Continental Illinois National Bank (taken over in part by the FDIC).
- First City Bank of Houston.
- Inter Republic Bank of Dallas (taken over by NCNB and FDIC).

THE FIVE CONDITIONS

Much of the credit codifying the following conditions for success must be attributed to the managing partner of Touche Ross, Edward A. Kangas, who prepared the conditions and warning signals for a seminar on strategy conducted for a *Business Week* conference.

In preparation for the seminar, Kangas surveyed a number of organizations to understand why strategy in many, if not most, organizations was never implemented. Kangas looked for systemic reasons why, in addition to management style and motivation for change, change did not occur as planned. Further, the persons who have built on the foundation of Kangas' work reasoned the five conditions that follow would be used to perform a strategic audit. The presence or absence of the five conditions could be examined, and if absent, they could be built into the process of strategic thinking for that particular business unit—thereby setting the stage for implementation from the beginning. As we have all learned, implementation really begins with the initiation of the process—not at its conclusion.

The five conditions that are essential for strategic thinking to be transformed into lasting competitive advantage are outlined briefly here and further described from the perspective of the client/customer service spectrum:

1. **Purpose**—There is a clear sense of purpose and an overall direction that is viable in the marketplace.
2. **Alignment**—Line management is aligned with the plan.

3. **Linkage**—Operating plans are linked to strategic plans.
4. **Implementation Tools**—Line management uses effective tools and techniques to implement changes called for in the plan.
5. **Anticipation**—Management anticipates the new set of problems caused by the shift in direction, and has established plans for coping with change.

Don Curtis, the former national director of the Touche Ross management consulting function, coined this phrase: "You don't solve problems in life, you trade them. You exchange the problems you have about which one naturally knows a great deal, for a new set of problems, the nature of which one can only anticipate." Both Kangas and Curtis demonstrated a keen insight into the complexities of implementation.

Rather than reading long paragraphs that illustrate each of the five conditions and their related warning signals, refer to Exhibits 9–1 through 9–5. They provide both the diagnostic indicators that depict the presence or absence of the conditions plus accompanying warning signals that are useful analogs to "audit" the indicators.

Left Side of the Spectrum

Condition 1
Purpose must be an integral part of professional enterprise. The professionals who form the interactive component of the service-delivery process form the purpose of the organization. They form the capability that is deployed to serve clients. There is no purpose without the collective involvement of the entire organization.

Condition 2
Alignment, just as with purpose, involves the commitment of the entire professional organization. It is possible, however, to have a purpose that is viable but an organization that is not necessarily aligned and committed. The failure of Finley Kumble, the international law firm, is a case in point. There was

nothing wrong with the purpose, however; the partners could not agree to implement that purpose.

Condition 3
Linkage. As Exhibit 9–3 illustrates, strategic action will not occur if there is no visible evidence that such action will be linked to the historic, observed, and adhered-to system of the organization. The linkage is like an automobile transmission. The transmission connects the engine to the drive shaft and the wheels. Similarly, the linkage between strategy and action must be present, and particularly visible to professionals on the left side of the spectrum.

Condition 4
Implementation tools, including task forces, project teams, and other temporary structures are essential to the change process and are effective because the professionals affected are in-cluded in designing the potential change. Because the profes-sionals *are* the service-delivery process, the success of implementation is a direct outcome of such participation.

Condition 5
Anticipation also requires the direct involvement of persons af-fected by any change in how the professionals practice. The realization by professionals that change implies risk, the un-known, and a new set of problems helps to smooth the bumps "that invariably occur when something new is attempted." A good example of the importance of anticipating new problems that surface when change is introduced is the failure of many mergers among professional services firms such as accounting, legal, consulting, investment-banking, advertising, and health-care organizations. Had integration problems been considered carefully in advance, either the mergers would have occurred more sensitively and smoothly or would never have been pursued.

Center of the Spectrum

Condition 1
Purpose is particularly critical for large, middle-market finan-cial services and retail organizations that are contemplating a

repositioning on the life cycle because of the risk of not getting the strategy right and not getting a second chance. Making a major move that will cause an organization to further
erode its position on the life cycle is a real possibility
unless the strategic-assessment and strategic-conclusions activities associated with process of strategic thinking are performed rigorously. Examples of organizations that seem to have
"gotten it right," in a difficult competitive environment are
The Limited and Disney. Both organizations have achieved
above-average outcomes notwithstanding major shifts in both
the fashion and entertainment industries because their process
of strategic thinking was rigorous, deep, and yielded focused,
viable purposes.

Condition 2
Alignment is a direct result of the management style referred
to as entrepreneurial innovation. Senior management "leads
the charge" in successful change—not the staff or planning organizations. This comment is not intended to downgrade the
critical importance of excellent staff work but to convey that
management leadership—especially senior management—internalize and deeply believe in where they are taking the
organization.

Condition 3
Linkage is critical to the implementation process because of
the power of communication. The entire organization gets the
message when senior management is willing to back up their
strategic action with direct linkages to the budget and compensation processes—two systems that determine and motivate behavior in most organizations.

Condition 4
Implementation tools are required for successful implementation, not only because the individuals who know what is happening become involved in the change process but because of
the need for additional resources to plan and manage successful change. Most organizations fail to make even the right
changes because managers do not have enough "arms and
legs." Slack resources are required to do the planning, run

pilot operations, or to convert existing operations. When such resources are not available, most managers revert to day-to-day management of existing operations.

Condition 5

Anticipation is important to the change process because regardless of how well change is planned, the unexpected always occurs. Here, anticipation as a condition for successful implementation conveys the thought that "can-do" attitudes of flexibility, innovation, and quick response to the unforeseen must be instilled in the organization. How unforeseen problems are accommodated and directions shifted, and how action and change are not interrupted mark successful implementation.

Right Side of the Spectrum

Condition 1

Purpose is an imperative at this point on the spectrum largely because of the huge capital investments and related risks required. The networks employed by Federal Express, UPS, and the transportation and telecommunications industries present competitive barriers and represent enormous financial risks. The strategic assessment, conclusions, and directions processes must lead to a *focused purpose* or the strategy will fail.

Condition 2

Alignment requires a well-disciplined, highly motivated, and committed "army" of line managers if change is to occur successfully. The regional quality-assurance organizations of McDonald's, Federal Express, and Marriott work closely with the interactive component of the service-delivery process to ensure that training occurs and that high standards of performance are maintained. Alternatively, an absence of such rigor causes many service failures.

Condition 3

Linkage at the right side of the spectrum, requires changes within the all-important process component to be made correctly. Since the process component contains the majority of activities in the service-value chain, those activities have to be directly linked to changes in strategy, including customer-service levels, cost targets, training budgets, incentive–bonus awards, etc. The life-insurance industry, particularly companies with captive-agency forces, are excellent illustrations of condition 3, in terms of linking changes in strategy, service mix, and so forth, to sales campaigns, commissions, and non-cash recognition for achieving sales targets for predetermined lines of service.

Condition 4

Implementation tools. As stated in Chapter 1, the risk of introducing new services is greater for a service enterprise than the introduction of new products is to an industrial organization as a direct result of the intangible nature of the "product." At this right side of the spectrum, there are a number of tools and techniques that may be used to mitigate against risk and to increase the success rate of change. Such tools and techniques include:

- Pilot projects or test sites that are separated from day-to-day operations, such as with the London Life "Wind Tunnel" project.
- Geographic regions of the country may be used to pilot new concepts, such as Sears' strategy of using the Southeast to launch the Discover Card.
- Project planning, control processes, and off-line information systems that are separated from the routine management-control processes.

There are many other tools as depicted in Exhibit 9–4.

A key implementation tool at this point on the spectrum is the management of expectations through effective senior management communication programs. Leonard D. Schaeffer, president and CEO of Blue Cross of California, made effective use of his President's Letter to keep all 5,000 members of his organization aware of what was happening during the three most turbulent years in the history of both the health-care industry and in the history of Schaeffer's organization. People know the facts and what to expect even during the days when the news was bad.

Condition 5

Anticipation is a critical condition at the right side of the spectrum as a direct result of having to manage, on a large scale, and "glitches" that can occur, particularly in the ever-important process component. Computer systems in the best of times will fail, and a backup system will be required to come on-line. Computer systems and the people who interact with them during times of stress and change will almost invariably fail and require extraordinary measures that have been planned in advance. For example, when the "Big Bang" occurred in the London financial industry in October of 1986, the securities-trading systems did not have the capacity to handle the greater-than-expected demand. It took weeks of intensive effort to modify both the software-and hardware-processing systems to accommodate a situation that might have been anticipated. Anticipation is not all about the exhaustive testing of every possible permutation in a computer process that any potential transaction may trigger. Such testing of billions of potential combinations is impossible. What is possible and necessary is that the management process and slack resources be available to handle the unknown when (not if) it occurs.

CONCLUSIONS

The three characteristics of the environment that must be in place for successful change to occur—an appropriate management style, the motivation for change, and the five conditions necessary for transforming strategy to action—merely set up the process of making changes. The presence of an appropriate environment is a necessary precondition; however, the environment alone changes nothing. Change occurs only when it is rigorously managed. Chapter 11 builds on the presence of the environment presented in this chapter and then describes how to manage change at various points on the client/customer service spectrum.

EXHIBIT 9–1
Transforming Strategy to Action

Condition 1: Purpose

Diagnostic Indicators	Warning Signals
• How explicit and clear is the purpose or mission statement and is it understood?	• "Our people know our mission—We don't need to write it down."
• To what extent are the needs of the marketplace identified and clearly defined?	• "Our information on the marketplace and our competitors is a little out of date."
• How well does the overall strategic direction address the needs of the marketplace?	• Declining market share.
• To what extent does the organization have the resources to carry out the strategic direction?	• "We are not sure just what resources are required."
• How well does the plan consider the competitive advantages and limitations of the organization?	• "This is basically a commodity business."

EXHIBIT 9–2
Transforming Strategy to Action

Condition 2: Alignment

Diagnostic Indicators	Warning Signals
• Who drives the planning process?	• Driven by a middle manager.
• What is the participation of line management?	• Line managers have limited participation.
• What is the role of planning staff in the planning process?	• Planning staff trying to *do* the plan.
• What is the intellectual understanding of the key elements of the plan?	• Managers refer to a document.
• What is the emotional buy-in or commitment to the plan and willingness to take responsibility?	• Tentative or questioning attitude.
• What priority is placed on planning relative to other management functions?	• "Our managers are too busy to plan."
• What is the elapsed time spent on the planning process?	• Process drags on longer than three months.
• To what extent are objectives, goals, and key decisions arrived at by consensus?	• Objectives are "slam-dunked."
• What has been the relative emphasis on the process versus the end result?	• Too much emphasis on end products.
• What is the nature of the planning documents and other end products?	• "The plan has two volumes."
• Does management believe the planning process is valuable?	• High noise level.
• What is the sense of cooperation and teamwork among line managers?	• "That's not in my area, I don't know what the plan is."
• What is the sense of relationship and how open is communication?	• Actions speak louder than words.

EXHIBIT 9–3
Transforming Strategy to Action

Condition 3: Linkage

Diagnostic Indicators	Warning Signals
• To what extent are objectives and expected results for the corporation disaggregated for the planning units' operating plans?	• Little connection of corporate and planning-unit objectives.
• What qualitative and quantitative operating targets exist?	• Operating targets do not reflect strategic direction.
• To what extent are participants in strategic planning active in planning?	• Line managers doing operating plans not involved in strategic planning.
• To what extent are accounting and information systems used to measure progress toward the goals?	• Managers are measured on something different than goals.
• To what extent is the compensation system linked to the goals?	• Compensation is independent of goals and plan.
• Do planning-unit operating plans reaggregate and "add up" to expected results on a consolidated basis?	• "There are too many variables and unknowns to reconcile the plans."

EXHIBIT 9–4
Transforming Strategy to Action

Condition 4: Implementation Tools

Diagnostic Indicators	Warning Signals
• What is the extent of management experience in implementing change?	• Little experience.
• To what extent is management present at the time of change?	• "I'll be traveling when we announce that change."
• How timely are required organizational changes implemented?	• Delays in making needed organizational change.
• To what extent does management use temporary "project organizations" to implement changes?	• Expecting line managers to take on the added work involved in addition to their normal job.
• How does management use "change agents" and "swat" teams to facilitate implementation?	• "We'll just tell the line managers what to change and they will figure out how to do it."
• How does management use off-line information systems to facilitate implementation?	• "We'll just change the existing systems to report this new information."
• How does management use action plans, workplans, and other project tools to implement changes?	• A tendency to make changes "by the seat of the pants."
• How does management handle anxiety, expectations, and politics during the time of change?	• "What anxiety?"
• To what extent does management use "off-line" rewards for success in implementing change?	• "Managing change is part of their job and considered in their normal rewards."
• What priority does implementation have?	• Missed deadlines.

EXHIBIT 9-5
Transforming Strategy to Action

Condition 5: Anticipation

Diagnostic Indicators	Warning Signals
• How attuned is management to the reality that problems are not solved but traded?	• "Once this change is in place, our troubles will be over."
• Does management appreciate the reality that unexpected problems always occur?	• "Our job is to test this new approach sufficiently to reach an error-free implementation."
• Do operating people appreciate the impact of the "experience curve" as applied to change?	• "Every change this place tries to make seems to go wrong."
• Do operating people realize that accommodating change is part of their job?	• "I'm not about to throw out the 'tried and true' until they prove that the new approach is better."
• Does management test the quality of implementation plans?	• "We will figure out the details as we go along."

CHAPTER 10

MANAGING CHANGE: A STRATEGY FOR IMPLEMENTATION

Chapter 9 discussed environment for change—the characteristics, management style, motivation and conditions for change that must be present for an organization to reposition itself on the life cycle and to emerge or reemerge as a refreshed, rejuvenated entity positioned to move along a new track. Chapter 9 set up the "what," and Chapter 10 deals with "how." The "what," as usual, is the much easier question to answer.

Let's focus the telescope of change on the characteristics of organizations that were cited in the previous chapter and elsewhere in this book—those that have and have not rejuvenated themselves and look for clues as to how some made it and some didn't. There are four issues:

1. A logic process for establishing a strategy for implementation.
2. The effective use of the client/customer service spectrum as a focal point for identifying the appropriate tools and techniques for making change.
3. An explicit set of change tools used in different ways at varying points on the spectrum.
4. Leadership of the organization that includes a willingness by individuals to trust their leader to show the way through the unknown paths of change.

ESTABLISHING AN
IMPLEMENTATION STRATEGY

The first of the four implementation issues is developing a logical, problem-solving process not unlike developing a strategy for a business unit. Such a process includes:

- A strategic assessment.
- Strategic conclusions.
- The strategic direction.

In establishing an implementation strategy, the problem-solving process incorporates:

A strategic assessment, including:

- What is the environment for change—as detailed in Chapter 4—perhaps including the outcome of a strategic audit of that environment?

Strategic conclusions, including:

- What needs to be done to deal with outcomes regarding the environment?
- Is sufficient change possible—can we get from here to there, and *is there a there*? In short, will we "break" the organization during our efforts to improve its position?

The strategic direction, including:

- Exactly how the task of change, in this particular and unique situation, will occur—what is our overall "game plan?"
- Which of the tools, techniques, and processes should we employ to implement our "game plan?"

THE TOOLS AVAILABLE FOR
MANAGING CHANGE

The second of the four issues in developing a strategy for implementation is the selection of proper tools. There are as many approaches to making changes as there are persons attempting change. However, in the interest of both brevity and to build upon excellent research, we have borrowed heavily from a note prepared for class discussion entitled *Managing Change* by Professor Jay W. Lorsch at the Harvard Business School.[1] At this point, it is useful to list the following major tools, techniques, and processes that are available to us, and then relate their potential uses in the following section at three points on the spectrum:

- Power.
- Process.
- Information.
- Communication.
- Consistency.
- Temporary structures.
- Pace.

THE CLIENT/CUSTOMER SERVICE SPECTRUM AS A FOCAL POINT

The third issue in developing a strategy for managing change—the *how*—includes an assessment of where an organization resides on the spectrum. We have employed the client/customer service spectrum as a major analytic tool to facilitate both the strategic-assessment and strategic-direction processes. When planning for a business unit, this same tool is equally useful in determining, at a macro- level, how change may be accomplished for a particular business unit.

Left Side of the Spectrum

Power
Almost disregarding what we classify as "pure service," the use of power and authority in a "top-down" sense, is an exercise

---

[1] Jay W. Lorsch, *"Managing Change,"* (Distributed by HBS Case Services). Copyright © 1974 by the President and Fellows of Harvard College. All rights reserved.

in futility and frustration. Professional people not only must be led rather than managed, they must feel as though they are sharing in all aspects of the change process. Groups of physicians, architects, engineers, accountants, consultants, attorneys, and restaurant chefs reject the use of top-down power. Power must be shared, not held, among the persons affected by change in a participative manner. Successful professional firms have discovered the "true" power belongs to the persons being led. Power, as a tool in the implementation of change, is either an ineffective or a negative instrument. Change cannot be "slam-dunked," as evidenced by failure at the Finley Kumble law firm, as well as the constant defections that occur as major investment-banking firms attempt to shift their strategic directions.

Process

Process, at the left side of the spectrum, is synonymous with the word "participative." Participative does not mean democratic. It does not imply leadership has no role or that all change must "bubble up" from the bottom before a shift in direction occurs. A participative process means that the individuals whose lives are at stake require a say in how change will occur. Participation in a power-sharing sense leads to consensus, which leads to commitment, which develops the energy, enthusiasm, and motivation for change. The participative process is not to be confused with the so-called "Japanese management style," which stresses much discussion and consensus as to what to do and how to do it, but does not share power. The participative process implies a time-consuming, never-ending series of meetings, memos, and minutia, but this does not have to be the case. A participative process can really move if organization members feel that they are in control of their destiny. Under the leadership of Pat Loconto, national director of management consulting at Touche Ross, the consulting activity of the firm has increased three-fold in growth of partners and profits in the past five years without the major defections and rebellion that occur in many large firms. Loconto has effectively used the power of the process in enlisting all the partners as part of the change process.

Information

To the professionals on the left side of the spectrum, information concerning the problem they are asked to solve, including the potential for success and the risk of failure, is an imperative. Such professionals, rather than terrified by the truth are motivated by the open, honest, two-way communication of information. The communication of fact-based, balanced information is essential to the participative process because such information not only confirms the need for change, but it reinforces the power-sharing intentions of leadership. Information—straightforward and honest—also reinforces what most talented, insightful professionals within an organization already know—that change is not only necessary but that their enlightened leadership is doing something about it. At the other extreme, when the "leadership" does not trust the organization with the truth, in the mistaken belief that the good people would "jump ship" if they knew the facts, the people who are required to make change are insulted.

Communication

At the left side of the spectrum, communication among professionals is not only a prerequisite—it is a condition for success. In addition, the communication must be "two-way." Professionals, as indicated earlier, are not "told what to do," or asked to do something in the absence of a two-way flow of information. This issue is both perceived and real. Perception is reality when it comes to the sensitive, empathetic, two-way communication of information. It is common for professionals to appear resistant to change, when in reality they believe that the proposed change is *dead wrong*. In addition, the professionals may be *dead right*. Even if the professionals are not completely correct regarding the potential risk of change, they *think* they are correct, and in this instance, perception equals reality. It is only through open, honest, *two-way* communication that both the leaders and their colleagues can know they are on the right track. The only kind of change that will occur in the absence of effective, two-way communication is what Leonard Schaeffer has referred to as "malicious compliance," that is, "I'll do what I'm told even if what I am told to do is wrong."

Consistency

Professionals who have choices will not follow "knee-jerk" leaders for long. The information of change must not only be sent and received, it must be consistent in content and impact to be internalized into a theme for change. If the correct direction has been selected for and with the organization, and if the appropriate approach to change management for the new organization direction has been selected, the "message" will only be creditable if delivered frequently and with the same language. The problems to be solved cannot change with either the weather or the latest in management fads, nor can the form or substance of the messages vary from day to day.

Temporary Structures

At the left side of the spectrum, change must become a part of the organizational fabric. Professionals will not change their behavior based upon the latest edition of the firm's policy and procedures manual.

Change must be "worked through" and internalized by the organization in a manner not perceived as devious or manipulative, but in a manner that allows professionals to arrive at their own conclusions concerning both the "what" and "how" of change.

Temporary structures such as task forces, project teams, or other short-term organizational forms are useful "change vehicles" if the leadership is effective and if the membership consists of professionals who are held in high esteem by their peers. Temporary structures not only serve the purpose of planning and managing change, the members, as they return to "home" organizations, carry the message of change with them. In effect, the task-force or project-team members become modern "apostles"—carrying and living the "message" of change by their actions.

Other productive uses of temporary structures include the transformation of the temporary structures into more permanent organizations to implement proposed changes. Such organizations may take on the form of "pilot" organizations, as with the Wind Tunnel project at London Life. Pilot organizations serve the critical purpose of testing changes in service concept;

demonstrating the workability and viability of the concept to the entire organization; and serving as a training ground for persons who will implement the concept throughout the entire organization.

The Touche Ross Financial Service Center, located in the World Financial Center of New York, is an example of a temporary organization that became permanent. Initially, a task force was established to determine the financial community's need for a focused, multidisciplined group of professionals to work on the complex issues concerning the changes occurring in global financial markets. The selected market segment was located at the left side of the spectrum. The task force studied current and prospective client needs at that point on the spectrum, established a strategic direction designed to serve those needs, and developed an implementation plan that converted the task force to a new Touche Ross practice office located in the World Financial Center. The Financial Service Center, with the leadership of Tom Presby, is a success, not only in its client-service role, but as a model for making change within the firm.

Pace

Earl Orser, from London Life, has provided numerous valuable lessons regarding the timing or pace of change. Earl has a fine-tuned "feel" for how quickly—or slowly—an organization may be "nudged" into different directions. The pace of change is a vital ingredient in Orser's management process and is the subject of every operating committee meeting and planning conference held at London Life. The London Life lesson is old and new. Change must be paced fast enough to be perceived as occurring by the entire organization and slow enough not to "run the engine off the tracks." Pace is, therefore, related to both the readiness and the ability of the organization to absorb change.

Center of the Spectrum

Power

Organizations that are most successful in serving the needs of clients and customers at the center of the spectrum include banks that serve middle-market corporate customers, retail department stores, and "white tablecloth" restaurants characterized as "people-sensitive." People are important at People's Bank, Nordstrom's, Wal-Mart, Marriott, Fleming, Fleet/Norstar Financial, and other competitively successful firms. The power of the organization is shared with the people at all organizational levels. None of the successful organizations we have yet studied on the spectrum have autocratic or bureaucratic leadership. While it is clear in all successful and some less successful organizations that strong leadership is in place; the winning organizations listen to their people, have empathy for their needs, and compete based upon the quality of their organization's people.

Process
When a focus on process takes precedence over a focus on action, an organization is in trouble at any point on the spectrum. Organizations at the center of the spectrum tend to be larger and have more levels of hierarchy, which run the risk of being "bound-up" by process or "paralysis by analysis." Studying an issue to death is an effective tactic to avoid implementation—as is malicious compliance.

Successful service organizations study issues appropriately, build consensus into the process, and make decisions. There is nothing worse than watching an organization miss opportunities to gain some form of opportunity because they couldn't or wouldn't take the risk and make a decision to move.

Bankers Trust serves as an excellent illustration of risk-taking and the management of change as the company sold its retail branch network, which was not a source of competitive strength, and built up its investment banking business—placing the bank among the largest and most profitable commercial banks in the country.

Information
Because organizations at the center of the spectrum are larger, with more layers than organizations found at the left side of the spectrum, information concerning how things work is both more difficult and more important to obtain. People at all levels, whether they are claims processors in an insurance

company, bank-branch managers, or commercial real estate brokers know their respective operations better than most senior managers. The successful implementation of change at the center of the spectrum depends on the information about current operations being understood by the entire organization prior to introducing proposed changes in those operations. Senior managers who listen to the people who implement the organization's work not only make more informed decisions, they avoid ill-informed mistakes. Senior managers who understand what people do are also awarded respect from the entire organization. People will make change more readily if they believe that their leaders know what they are doing. Conversely, the behavior that we related earlier—"malicious compliance"—sets in when the organization doesn't believe in or trust leadership.

Communication

Two-way communication may be as important at the center of the spectrum as it is at the left side of the spectrum. Even potentially bad news, such as reductions in force, geographic relocations, or other changes to the status quo must be communicated truthfully and quickly because, for the most part, the truth is not as bad as rumors that occur in a vacuum. The greater the amount of information that senior management shares with all levels of the organization, the smoother the implementation of change.

Consistency

The "game plan" can't change every day. A few, well-thought-out messages, consistently applied, often are the difference between success and failure. This is not to imply that organization plans must be simple to be understood or communicated with consistency. Once the plans for change are thought through, they must be communicated in the same manner, that is, using the same words, on a consistent basis.

Temporary Structures

Large organizations found at the center of the spectrum, if they are successful in implementing change, use temporary structures as a prerequisite for success. The intangible nature of the service, coupled with the need for consensus by the people who are affected, requires that changes be tested by the persons involved before institution-wide acceptance is possible.

The Prudential provides an excellent example of using task forces. The Prudential is a huge, fast-growing, diversified, successful institution that could be subject to "hardening of the arteries" that large organizations are susceptible to. The Prudential has made change not only a way of life, but a basis of competition. The Prudential, under the leadership of Chairman Robert Winters and his predecessors, created an environment of trust in the organization's leadership—a firm psychological contract. Within the terms of the trust-based psychological contract, task forces are chartered, formed, fulfill their role, and disband. Task forces have created, managed, and implemented much of the change that has occurred at The Prudential over the past 20 years. Membership on a task force is a vital part of the reward system at The Prudential with the title of a particular task force often being the person's name. Talk about motivation for success!

Pace
Managing pace is just as critical at the center of the spectrum as it is on the left, if not more so. As John Teets of Greyhound pointed out, once a large organization has lost its trust in management, its culture, and is "broken," the old rules are gone for good. A search must begin for a new, untried process that may have greater problems than the system it replaces. An attempt to "force" the pace of change that is greater than the absorption rate of the organization will, in many instances, "break" the organization that the leadership attempts to help.

Pace is, of course, dependent on all of the tools, techniques, and processes that have been discussed in the foregoing paragraphs. For successful change to occur at the center of the spectrum, it must be done right—the first time. Large organizations are perishable, vulnerable, and, once on a path, sometimes called the "death spiral," their course is often irreversible. A quick look at the former great names of the Wall Street investment community serve as vivid examples.

Pace may occur more quickly when the information concerning the contemplated change is reasonably complete and even quicker when little resistance is anticipated.

Right Side of the Spectrum

Power

If the use of top-down power has its place anywhere along the spectrum, it might seem appropriate at the far-right, near-product point. Among successful service companies at the far right, and word "power" is never used. Power might be available as a potentially quick means of making change in an authoritarian or autocratic sense at the far right, but in our research, the top-down application of power is seldom found in successful organizations. Rather, power is used to create policy, and policy becomes the vehicle for change and the ultimate basis of competition.

The Fleming Companies, cited earlier for their pioneering work in human-resource strategy, have made dozens of wholesale grocery acquisitions on their journey toward becoming the largest wholesale-grocery distributor in the United States. Fleming has a competitive wholesale-grocery distribution system known as FOODS (Fleming On-Line Operational Distribution System), which represents the "Fleming way" of doing business—a process that places a premium on the quality and productivity of the service that the company provides. Fleming has a policy of converting its acquisitions to FOODS as a vehicle for integrating the new organization as a division within the overall network. FOODS is a vehicle for making change through the conversion of power to policy. Fleming also has a policy of *not* forcing an acquired company to implement FOODS until and unless the management of the new division sees it as fitting. Fleming has the power to make change, but it uses that power selectively through policy.

Other organizations at the right side of the spectrum that use power discreetly as a means of creating change include: Disney, National Bank of Detroit, Citibank, H&R Block, McDonald's, American Express, La Quinta, Dun and Bradstreet, and Dow Jones. Each organization shares the common characteristics of a rapidly changing environment, fierce competition, and a requirement to move quickly.

Process

At the right side of the spectrum, power converts to process quite well, provided the policy is sound in the first place. Some observers of McDonald's and H&R Block contend that how they manage change—whether the change is in the form of consumer taste or changes in the tax law—forms the real basis for their competitive success. Certainly no two organizations have made change any more effectively.

The characteristics of the change process that McDonald's and H&R Block organizations share, beyond consistent policy, include extensive "laboratory-like" testing and other sampling processes that give their field organizations confidence in knowing that the changes they are asked to make will work. The two organizations share a history of field involvement in such tests so that their field organizations trust headquarters' policy and process.

At this right side of the spectrum, process does not mean consensus-building or participation in the change process by persons who will be affected by the contemplated change. Process at the right side of the spectrum means an assurance on management's part that they have done their homework and that the change will be *done right*!

Information

Information concerning what happens at the headquarters level is strangely not a critical issue at the right side of the spectrum *if* trust in policy and process are present in the field. If such trust is not present, information becomes a political "chip" to be bargained. When trust is present, information sharing is required primarily at the local or field location. People at the local, "store-front" level are primarily concerned about how contemplated changes will impact them, their families, and their well-being.

A good example of the requirement for locally-communicated change centers around changes in compensation systems for field employees. No amount of top-down, headquarters-driven communication will replace the efforts of a branch manager to share information one-on-one with employees.

Communication
The old adage, "I would have been more brief, if I had had more time" applies here. Brief, carefully thought-out imagery is essential in communicating with large, field-driven service organizations. "The medium is the message," according to Marshall McLuhan. Whether the medium is printed employee annual reports or video tapes that communicate a strategic theme, an image of quality, customer service, and the role of the employee in the delivery of both add value not only to the service delivered, but to the self-worth of the person delivering that service.

Consistency
As critical as the message is, the consistency with which it is delivered is even more important. The message of change must be reinforced using the same vocabulary to a point where the message is woven into the organizational fabric.

The customer-service message at American Express is a good example. The customer-service representatives at American Express are the elite company representatives. They have become so—relative to their competition—because they have been educated with that theme for a generation. American Express representatives know their product, which is changing constantly, communicate the product features articulately because of the consistent message delivered to them—"that they are the best."

Temporary Structures
Temporary structures, other than in testing the service-delivery concept, do not seem as pervasive a mechanism for change at the right side of the spectrum as at other points. Being sent from the field to test a concept or to "brainstorm" a problem and its solution may be useful only if the headquarters organization honestly seeks the input and is prepared to act on it. Otherwise, such involvement in task forces, committees, or project teams does more harm than good. Temporary structures are not required as long as there is trust in organiza-

tional leadership. If the trust is not present, the formation of a temporary structure is perceived as devious.

Pace

Large, field-driven organizations can and do move quickly, as evidenced by the emergence of K mart as the nation's second-largest retailer in a period of less than 10 years. Wal-Mart has experienced similar profitable growth in a short time.

Pace, in large organizations, is not as constrained by having to "bring everyone on board," as is the case with organizations at the left or center of the spectrum. Pace is constrained by having to "get it right."

There are numerous instances of organizations that did not get the pace of change "right," and the reasons vary with the number of institutions—just like the situation with the "winners." The common thread, as one might expect, is moving too slow. Change, like nature, can't stand a vacuum and, as a result, when an organization is poised for change and seems unable to "capture the moment," the momentum is lost. The good people who can manage change are also lost.

LEADERSHIP OF THE ORGANIZATION

The last of the four major issues addressed in an organization's efforts to develop a strategy for implementation is leadership. Throughout this book have been actual examples of organizations that have emerged or reemerged on their respective life cycles as new, vibrant competitors. Such successful competitors have effective leaders—men or women around whom the organization could rally and move forward. Interestingly, the leadership of organizations unable to keep up or to change sufficiently are seldom mentioned. Those faceless, nameless managers who headed unsuccessful organizations are seldom remembered.

In researching successful companies—organizations that have achieved a sustainable competitive advantage—a leader, by name, is always identifiable and associated with change. The role of effective leadership, therefore, is a critical factor, not only in the ongoing management of an enterprise, but perhaps even more importantly, in the implementation of change. We have yet to see a successful organization that did not have a successful leader at the helm.

Regarding the issues of change, the word *trust* is often associated with the word *leadership*. A leader who has earned the trust of those he or she is leading is often able to create and manage change even when the course of action is not clear. The rank and file will follow a trusted leadership knowing that the leader will always put the interests of those being led ahead of his or her agenda.

It is useful to identify organizations that have emerged or reemerged and have achieved lasting competitive advantage with the individuals who caused such change. Such leaders are not necessarily loved in a hero-worshiping sense, but they are trusted and respected. Undoubtedly, we will have left out names, however, associating successful service companies with

Institution	Leader
Albertsons	Joseph A. Albertson
American Hospital Supply	Carl D. Bays
Automatic Data Processing (ADP)	Frank R. Lautenberg
BancOne	John G. McCoy
Capital Holding	Thomas C. Simons
Citibank	Walter B. Wriston
Dayton-Hudson	Bruce B. Dayton
Fleming	Ned N. Fleming
Holiday Inn	Kemmons Wilson
McDonald's	Raymond A. Kroc
Merrill Lynch	Charles E. Merrill
Morgan Stanley	Robert H. B. Baldwin
National Bank of Detroit	Robert M. Surdam
Nordstrom's	John W. Nordstrom
Prudential	Donald McNaughton
Touche Ross & Co.	Russell E. Palmer
United Parcel Service (UPS)	Paul Oberkotter
Wal-Mart	Sam Walton

their leaders illustrates the point; it does not create an all-inclusive honor roll. Therefore, we have only identified leaders who are recognizable, retired, and in some cases deceased.

Our list could go on, particularly among leaders cited throughout this book. We hope our point is made not just in terms of people who became famous, but also to acknowledge leaders who were effective but unsung heroes within their organizations. Such leaders have one characteristic in common—a focus on people and clients/customers.

CONCLUSIONS

Organizations revitalize themselves or reposition themselves on the life cycle through the effective management of change—and change must be managed.

The key to emergence or reemergence is perspective. The start-up entrepreneur has only one perspective—an outward focus *on the customer.* It is only after the emerging company matures, specializes, and hires nonentrepreneurs that a different perspective emerges—*inward on the process.*

The power of the inward-process focus is greater than the often weaker voice of the customer. The power of the inward focus must be transformed into the power of a customer focus for the mature institution to change its position on the life cycle and reemerge as a vibrant, competitive force.

The Fleming Companies' chairman, Dean Werries, put this issue of perspective in focus when he described Fleming's success in merging smaller voluntary wholesale grocery chains into the Fleming network. Werries points out that such organizations survive by placing their focus outward on customers, a characteristic shared with the Fleming culture. Another examination of the Fleming organization chart (Exhibit 7–1) illustrates this point.

If only everyone within an organization had a customer to serve.

CHAPTER 11

"PAINT THE MOUNTAIN": OUR VISIONS SUSTAIN US

Dr. Anthony Athos, a former professor at Harvard, inspired much of our thinking about the "soft" side of business a decade ago at a Harvard-sponsored advanced management program— Managing Organizational Effectiveness. While much of the discussion dealt with behavioral change and was quite useful, Athos' thesis dealt with the issues that sustain us and cause us to grow—our visions and dreams. In service businesses, at any point on the client/customer service spectrum, the concept of a shared vision of what the business can be is the basis for all management processes. The dreams or visions provide the motivation, enthusiasm, spark, and spirit of entrepreneurial innovation that attract clients/customers and professionals/employees/associates that build great firms. In today's world of quantative analysis and controllers, talk of dreams and vision seems almost out of sync; however, when the *real* basis of competitive advantage is people, a shared vision on the part of those people forms a timeless competitive barrier.

Professor Athos characterized an organization motivated by vision as having a *"superordinate goal."* In this context, the term is used to describe a timeless, overriding goal that transcends all other business strategies or objectives. Russell E. Palmer, dean of The Wharton School at the University of Pennsylvania, and a former managing partner of Touche Ross, described a superordinate goal for the firm as "be best." That goal was ideal for many of us because we could translate it from individual perspectives into personal goals and still behave consistently with the firm's expectations.

Donald W. Jennings, one of the founding partners of Touche Ross' management-consulting practice, coined the phrase and the task—"paint the mountain": painting the mountain, by persons who also had to climb the mountain, provided enormous inspiration and motivation to a group of young professionals a quarter of a century ago which, with careful nurturing by a succession of effective leaders, resulted in the building of one of the most successful general management consulting firms in the world. Jennings understood leadership versus management long before the "books were written." He knew instinctively that, with proper coaching, people who could come to their own conclusions never needed to be told what to do—that is, be managed. Jennings led people not only by helping them to "paint the mountain" but by helping them to climb the mountain. The Jennings legacy has not only sustained the Touche Ross management-consulting practice over 25 years, but it has formed a timeless basis of future competition. Jennings made a person feel as if you could accomplish anything! Consequently, many of us did things we never thought we could do.

WHY IS THE CONCEPT OF VISION ESSENTIAL?

The research conducted about the underlying themes that seem to "track" with service firms that have achieved long-term competitive advantage reveals firms and people who are motivated by a vision. The use of the word *vision* in this instance is different than used in earlier chapters when vision was used in conjunction with a strategic direction or mission. The use of vision here regards the concept of a superordinate goal. A goal that people may internalize on their own that becomes the gyroscope for both the person and the organization—giving both direction and inspiration.

Sam Walton, the former chairman, CEO, and founder of Wal-Mart Stores, put it this way, "being friendly to customers, tough with suppliers, inspirational to employees, extremely profitable to shareholders"[1]

The concept and the reality of a vision as the internal gyroscope of both the service individual and the service organization has, over the long term, the fundamental difference between a product and a service. The product is a rallying point for even the most innovative and entrepreneurial start-up product-based firm and continues throughout the life of both the product and the firm. The famous start-up ventures at Apple Computer, Hewlett-Packard, Microsoft, and Sun Microsystem were driven by the vision of their founders and early colleagues. However, the continuing evolution of these and other product-oriented companies witnessed the transition of that early vision to the product and product line.

In the absence of the tangible product, the vision of service, in the successful enterprise, must transcend the early start-up service concept and be ingrained in the attitudes and behavior of each person within the organization if long-term competitive advantage is to be attained. Examples of the imperative of an internalized vision (versus a product-focused vision) of service on the entire service organization may be found, in addition to Wal-Mart, by examining competitively successful enterprises at each of the three points on the client/customer service spectrum:

The Left Side of the Spectrum

- Bankers Trust
- Four Seasons Hotels.
- Goldman-Sachs.
- Morgan Guarantee Bank.
- Morgan Stanley Group.
- Neiman Marcus.

---

[1]Wal-Mart: Will It Take Over the World?, *Fortune* (January 30, 1989), pp. 52–61.

The Center of the Spectrum

- The Limited.
- Marriott Hotels.
- Nordstrom's.
- Wells-Fargo Bank.
- United Parcel Service (UPS).

The Right Side of the Spectrum

- American Express.
- Automatic Data Processing (ADP).
- Federal Express.
- H&R Block.
- K Mart.
- McDonald's.
- Toys "Я" Us.

Admittedly, these firms represent a small sample of the "outliers" found in a few industry categories. However, it is the exceptions to the average that lead to lasting competitive advantage. Failure to achieve the shared vision of service excellence at best relegates many firms to the gray, nondescript, middle-of-the-road business and at worst describes failure.

THE CHARACTERISTICS OF AN ORGANIZATION DRIVEN BY VISION AND SUPERORDINATE GOALS

The following major themes—those characteristics shared by all first-rate companies and by many successful industrial organizations—will be briefly described in the following paragraphs:

- Trust and mutual respect.
- A sense of ownership/partnership.
- Leadership versus management.
- Tolerance of differences.
- The organization as a verb.

- People versus position.
- Innovation/risk.

Trust and Mutual Respect

This theme was explored at some length in the context of the human-resource strategy. The theme is reiterated here because without trust and mutual respect among service professionals and associates, nothing is possible in the way of a shared vision or superordinate goals. Apolitical behavior (i.e., doing what is "right" for the entire organization), is a prerequisite to creating an environment where anything is possible.

The question remains—how is an environment of trust and mutual respect achieved? Certainly such attitudes emanate from the organization's leaders—both positively and negatively. The leaders of successful organizations trust the motives and behavior of the people whose lives and careers are entrusted to them. Such leaders actively and visibly promote feelings of trust and mutual respect among members of the organization. Selfish, political, and generally negative behavior are visibly not tolerated by the leadership. Success in creating the required environment is characterized by an absence of one individual or group "putting down" another individual or group to build themselves up. In the final analysis, mutual respect and trust are present when such behavior is visibly rewarded and absent when visible rewards are absent.

A Sense of Ownership/Partnership

We cannot all be owners or partners in service enterprises. Some organizations, unlike the Fleming Companies, do not describe their employees as associates. What we can do, however, as leaders of service organizations, is to create a sense of ownership and partnership in the business on the part of all colleagues.

As was the case with describing superordinate goals or visions, the definitions become quite "fuzzy." The difficulty in describing feelings that seem to defy description, however, shouldn't deter us. Feelings of ownership and partnership go beyond the legal definitions of those terms. The difference between the behavior of a colleague who feels like an owner/partner and that of an employee who has a job is the difference in competitive results between firms.

At this point, it may be useful to refer back to the position of an organization on its life cycle to further describe the differences in behavior between people who share a proprietary interest in the enterprise and those who have a job maintaining that enterprise.

Organizations, at any point on the client/customer service spectrum, which are in their early developmental phase, almost intuitively behave as though their corporate life depends entirely on acquiring and keeping early customers or clients. Customer/clients are treated more differently at this point on the life cycle than at any other point.

Organizations at the more mature or declining phases of the life cycle have difficulty in sustaining that early sense of ownership/partnership in the business. Parenthetically, this is a reason why they find themselves at the mature or declining state of their corporate lives. In many conversations with partners and clients, the observation has been made that we treat clients that we have brought into the firm differently than clients inherited from other partners. The question remains—how does a firm sustain that early life-cycle sense of ownership/partnership?

In our experience with firms that have maintained a sense of ownership/partnership among their colleagues, regardless of their location on the client/customer service spectrum, the following are consistent themes:

• Actual ownership of shares/options or other evidence that the firm's performance will make a difference in the individual's direct or indirect compensation (i.e., the sense of ownership/partnership on the part of the individuals who have become involved with leveraged buyouts or master limited partnerships, has increased subsequent to the transaction).

• Implementation of programs designed to treat existing clients or customers as though they were prospective clients or customers seems to reemphasize the commitment on the part of the entire organization to the entrepreneurial spirit of the original enterprise.

• A continual commitment, on the part of all members, to growth of the business. *Growth*, in this sense of the word, is intended to mean "growth for growths' sake." Organizations that are not growing are dying, in terms of their market presence and their entrepreneurial spirit.

Leadership versus Management

It is probably true that effective management is synonymous with effective leadership. Leadership is the key to the issue of channeling and focusing organizational resources toward attaining the vision that the group has created or the mountain that they have painted.

Effective leaders derive their power from whom they lead as opposed to the hierarchal position they occupy in the firm's structure. As long as leaders remember where their source of power comes from, and that power is fragile and temporary, leadership is effective. The leaders in service firms serve persons who have entrusted the obligation to lead on them.

Great firms are invariably created and sustained by great leaders (versus great managers). The distinction is important when successful service companies are compared to less successful companies. It is difficult to name a successful service institution that is not characterized by superior leadership.

Tolerance of Differences

Great firms, businesses that are driven by a vision, are also characterized by their absence of a "mold" or single set of behavioral characteristics. Granted that the common denominator among all great firms is talent (versus skill), the similarities stop there. Great firms tolerate the differences among people, indeed, they encourage such differences. Great firms seek out and promote "star quality" (versus the star system), and star quality comes in different packages.

The Organization as a Verb

The current managing partner of Touche Ross, Ed Kangas, has often characterized the ideal professional-services firm as consisting of people who are action-oriented—verbs—rather than nouns. This imagery is useful for describing people on the move, people who are builders versus maintainers, and an environment of enthusiasm and excitement.

The imagery of the organization as a verb also connotes a "flat" versus hierarchal organizational structure—one that Ed Kangas defines as "field-driven"—an absence of bureaucracy and a sense of leadership versus traditional executive behavior. In fact, one of Kangas' first moves after being elected as managing partner was to disband the so-called "executive committee," a committee consisting solely of New York-based partners in staff roles, and replacing it with a committee of mainly field leaders. In addition, the name of the executive office was changed to that of national office, and the term *staff* was dropped in favor of *colleagues*.

Mountains are painted and climbed by people of all ages, genders, sexualities, nationalities, and races who have one thing in common—they climb mountains. They don't send their staff.

People versus Positions

Organizations on the move are led by people—not positions on an organizational chart. Since successful organizations are characterized as having highly talented people of diverse backgrounds, each person in a leadership role brings something different to that role than either the former or succeeding person in that role. The characteristics of the role will change with the incumbent, and such change should be encouraged.

Great firms with great leaders do not use the positions in an organizational chart to define who does what and who has what authority or responsibility; they permit the dynamics of the human organization to answer those questions and to change the questions and answers regularly.

Innovation/Risk

Innovation is such a key ingredient in creating and sustaining an organizational vision that it was described in Chapter 6 as a separate area of strategic action. Innovation and its companion—risk—are further highlighted in this chapter to emphasize their critical importance to the success of service companies.

Innovation and risk-taking also belong in this chapter because they can't be defined or measured and may only be sensed by their presence or absence. Tony Athos used the phrase "hard drives out the soft," meaning that the requirement on the part of managers, often accountants, to justify, quantify, measure, and control innovative ideas and risk-taking often drives out the individuals and ideas necessary to sustain the institution's vision.

Innovation and risk are at the heart of service-institution competitive advantage whether it be marketing and products; technology and operations; or human-resource initiatives. All great service firms are innovative and reward risk-takers.

How Is "Buy-In" to a Service Vision Achieved?

The characteristics indicated above do not just "happen." On the other hand, such visions and superordinate goals are not "managed." Clearly, the leaders named in this chapter had a vision and instilled that vision in their organizations. The question is—how?

In our consulting and other research, the organizations and leaders that we have observed have knowingly or unknowingly communicated their values and visions by personal example. The actions of their leaders spoke louder than any words they may have uttered. Such actions—call it leadership—were directly transmitted to the persons being led. No amount of memos, plaques, slogans, or other public pronouncements communicated with the power of personal behavior demonstrated by the leaders. There are no simple answers to complex questions.

CONCLUSIONS

Service companies, according to John Teets at Greyhound, compete with each other based on how well each individual in the institution deals with his or her client/customer. John Teets also feels that a major difference between service and industrial strategy is this same characteristic—be close to the customer. Service-sector strategy begins and ends with the client/customer as contrasted to the functional specialization required to operate with consistent quality and productivity in a product-based industrial organization.

The vision that service-sector organizations create must *first* focus on the client/customer and the needs of that client/customer and *then* on how the service organization may best fill those needs. Service organizations differ dramatically from their industrial counterparts on this dimension. Most industrial organizations and some distribution organizations first focus on what they can make or buy and then on whom to sell their product.

Great service firms, driven by a vision, know exactly whom they wish to serve and what it will take to be successful. Regardless of the point on the client/customer service spectrum, great service companies instill in their members an awareness of the shared vision and a commitment to the excellence required to achieve that vision.

It is our visions that sustain us.

APPENDIX

THE SUSTAINABLE PERFORMANCE INDEX

The Sustainable Performance Index (SPI) was developed by colleagues at Touche Ross and Braxton Associates who were acknowledged in the preface to this work. In addition, Liz Carducci, Mike DeCavalcante, and Christine Russo of the New York management-consulting practice of Touche Ross "burned the midnight oil" toiling over a "hot computer" in their efforts to provide statistical and mathematical credibility to our efforts.

The Sustainable Performance Index (SPI) was developed to test our long-standing hypothesis that organizations providing high-quality service productively are rewarded by superior returns financially and economically. Of even greater importance is the assumption that such returns are sustained. Successful service companies, therefore, are characterized as having achieved a sustained competitive advantage, over time, on an economic basis as well as superior financial performance. For this book, economic performance relates to shareowner value while financial results relate to the internal measures of performance that we have termed the SPI.

THE INDEX

The underlying philosophy of the SPI is that a measure of a company's performance should reflect good performance for more than just a calendar year of time, and that the method for selecting a performance measure should be market-based and rigorous. For these reasons, the SPI measures performance over a seven-year period; furthermore, the components of the SPI are financial measures that have a demonstrated relationship to the market value of a firm's shares.

The ranking is based on a firm's demonstrated performance over a seven-year period. Performance is based on a firm's compound annual growth rate in sales, and its average profit margin over that seven-year period.

The SPI was designed to identify firms in the service industry that have been top or bottom performers over a sustained period, rather than as a complete analysis of the factors contributing to share-owner value. We do not claim that it is the only approach, but that it is a straightforward and easy-to-apply technique for identifying top or bottom performers. Our next step, which is a subject of potential further investigation, is to determine whether common causal characteristics help distinguish between sustained good or poor performance. We expect that the characteristics described in Chapter 8 will be more prevalent in a list of top performers and will be lacking in the bottom performing companies.

Construction of the SPI

The selection of a seven-year rather than a six- or eight-year measurement period was arbitrary. We felt that four years of performance history was an absolute minimum. Seven-year averages and average growth rates were used because many data bases retain only the most recent years of history.

Our belief that only "market-based" performance measures should be included in the SPI is a free-market concept. Taken to an extreme, one can argue that the perfect market-based measure is a firm's shareowner value, and that measuring the growth rate in shareowner value over a prolonged period is the simplest way of assessing sustained good management.

Though theoretically true, in actuality, market-price data suffers from point-in-time measurement distortions. Measurement distortions arise because stock prices are volatile—reflecting market swings until an equilibrium is reached. For example, in our data base through 1987, Southland Corporation is ranked number 1 in our index of retailers based on market value; however, it is ranked number 37 out of 38 retailers in the SPI ranking. The reason is simple. The day that Southland's stock price was measured coincided in time with speculation in the stock.

The SPI is used in combination with market value as an indicator to screen for those companies that exhibit the best sustained performance. Ranking in the SPI is based on the company's six-year compound annual growth rate in sales (seven years of data), and its profit margin averaged over the last six years. The company having a ranking of 1 in the index has the highest combined growth in sales, and average profit-margin performance over the last seven years. Correspondingly, the company at the bottom of the index has the worst combined sales growth and profit margin performance over the last seven years. Sales growth and average profit margin were selected as components of the SPI because our analysis of operating and financial variables showed them to be the strongest indicators of a company's economic value. Inclusion on the list of top or bottom performers required that a company be ranked at the top or bottom of the SPI *and* at the top or bottom of the market value ranking.

Determining Index Components

Selecting financial results that "tracked" with economic performance required a fair amount of testing various hypotheses, including:

- High compound annual growth rate in sales (CAGR SALES).
- High average net income divided by sales (AVG NI/SALES).
- High average annual-growth rate in net income (AAGR NI).
- High average return on assets (ROA).
- High average post-tax cash flow ROA (CFROA).
- High average return on equity (ROE).
- High compound annual-growth rate in assets (CAGR ASSETS).
- High average operating earnings divided by sales (AVG EBIT/ SALES).
- High average operating earnings divided by assets (AVG EBIT/ ASSETS).
- High average annual-growth rate in EBIT (AAGR EBIT).

Indicators such as market to book value were excluded from the analysis because they are highly correlated with market value. Variables such as dividend payments and regularity of dividend payments were tested, but were found to be only marginally correlated with market value. This result is most likely explained by the large capital appreciation of equity in the last few years, causing dividends to be a relatively small percentage of total return.

Of the ten "financial performance" hypotheses tested, all showed some correlation with the economics of shareowner value. The correlations are presented in Table 1. Of these variables, several were highly correlated with one another. Table 2 shows the correlation among several of the variables. In general, earnings before interest and taxes (EBIT) and net-income variables (NI) had a correlation factor of more than .8; sales and asset variables had a correlation factor of more than .85.

Our analysis showed that although both CAGR ASSET and CAGR SALES helped explain market value, CAGR SALES was a better explanatory variable for both banks and nonbanks. Although both AVG EBIT/SALES and AVG NI/SALES contributed to explaining market value, AVG NI/SALES was a stronger explanatory variable for both banks and nonbanks.

One difference between banks and nonbanks was the correlation between AVG EBIT/ASSETS and MKT VALUE. As might be ex-

TABLE 1
Independent Variables—Correlation with Market Value

	Correlation with Market Value (excluding banks)	Correlation with Market Value (banks only)
AAGR NI	.5127	.6389
CAGR SALES	.4963	.7310
CAGR ASSETS	.4797	.6792
ROA	.4794	.6538
CFROA	.4749	.6252
ROE	.4548	.6416
AVG NI/SALES	.4498	.5638
AAGR EBIT	.4074	.5850
AVG EBIT/SALES	.4052	.4744
AVG EBIT/ASSETS	.3685	.6077

TABLE 2
Correlation between Variables

Correlated Independent Variables		Correlation Factors (excluding banks)	Correlation Factors (banks only)
CFRA	AAVG EBIT/ASSETS	.9072	.9482
CAGR ASSET	CAGR SALES	.8851	.8164
ROA	ROE	.8625	.9500
AVG EBIT/SALES	AVG NI/SALES	.8146	.9434
CFROA	ROA	.7969	.9044
ROE	AVG NI/SALES	.7670	.8346
CFROA	AVG EBIT/SALES	.7340	.6090
ROE	AVG EBIT/ASSETS	.7240	.9216

pected, AVG EBIT/ASSETS for banks is more strongly correlated with market value than for nonbanks. However, we believe that changes in the banking industry make asset base a less meaningful measure of bank performance than earnings. For example, banks are actively reducing their asset bases and generating fee income by securitizing assets. Furthermore, it is widely recognized that a growing percentage of bank assets (on which income is earned) is off balance sheet. Because of these factors, we believe that AVG EBIT/ SALES is a more meaningful explainer of bank performance than is the traditional AVG EBIT/ASSETS variable. Table 2 provides additional detail on the highly correlated independent variables.

After eliminating variables that were highly correlated, to avoid double counting in the final index, the most critical of the "financial performance" variables were:

- CAGR SALES.
- AVG NI/SALES.

These two variables were tested as independent variables in a multiple regression analysis using cross sectional data; the dependent variable in the regression was the growth in market value (MKTVALUE). MKTVALUE was constructed by multiplying the number of diluted shares outstanding at the end of the calendar year times the market price per share at the same point in time. The cross sectional data, excluding banks, contained data on 141 companies. Regressions were run using the two independent variables. The results of the regressions are presented in Table 3.

In addition to the basic regressions described in Table 3, the same series of regressions were run after the data were purged of outliers created by the mergers and acquisitions activity that occurred in 1987. Three companies were removed from the cross-sectional data because it was confirmed that their stock-price data were distorted in 1987. The three companies removed from the sample were:

- Caesar's World.
- Primerica.
- Southland.

The results of the regression analysis, after eliminating the three outliers, is presented in Table 4. As seen in the results, eliminating the three outliers made only a marginal difference in the regression analysis. The stability of the regression equation is a result of the large number of companies in the data base. The elimination of the outliers had a greater impact on the industry-specific analysis. We also ran regressions with banks included in the sample; results reinforced the data presented in Tables 3 and 4.

The Cross-Sectional Data Base

Table 5 shows the ranked data used for the regression analysis; Table 6 presents the "raw" unranked data for the same companies and variables. Tables 5 and 6 are organized by industry group. The data base is comprised of companies in the 1988 Fortune Service 500— excluding transportation companies, telecommunication companies, insurance companies (except companies grouped as diversified financial), savings and loan institutions, and utilities. In all, 300 companies are represented in the Fortune Service 500 list for the industries in-

TABLE 3
Regression Results (including outliers)

	"t" Statistics	
Regression Function	CAGR SALES	AVG NI/SALES
MKVALUE =		
f(CAGR SALES, AVG NI/SALES)	4.58	3.41
f(CAGR SALES)	7.00	N/A
f(AVG NI/SALES)	N/A	6.17

TABLE 4
Regression Results (excluding outliers)

	"t" Statistics	
Regression Function	CAGR SALES	AVG NI/SALES
MKTVALUE =		
f(CAGR SALES, AVG NI/SALES)	4.91	3.32
f(CAGR SALES)	7.36	N/A
f(AVG NI/SALES)	N/A	6.21

cluded in the analysis. Of the 300 companies, 218 are represented in our data base, including:

- 35 retail companies.
- 73 diversified service companies.
- 33 diversified financial companies.
- 77 banks.

Table 7 identifies the 82 companies that are on the Fortune Service 500 list but that are excluded from our data base. Table 7 also identifies why each company was excluded. In general, a Fortune Service 500 company is excluded if it experienced a major restructuring in the last seven years, resulting in missing data during the seven-year period that we have analyzed. Data for the retail, diversified services, and diversified financial companies were obtained from the Compustat on-line data base and supplemented with data from the Datext data base and hardcopy research. Bank data were compiled using Sheshunoff's banking data available from the Datext on-line data base. Compound annual-growth rates are based on data from 1982 to 1988; averages are based on data from 1983 to 1988.

In addition to industry groupings taken from the Fortune Service 500 list, we independently compiled a list of the top 46 life insurance parent companies and the top 50 property and casualty companies. These data were taken from Best's Insurance Report. Rankings, raw data, and exclusions for these groupings of insurance companies are also included in Tables 5, 6, and 7.

The Sustainable Performance Index (SPI)

The SPI is based on the regression results previously described. The index uses as its components, rankings based on:

- CAGR SALES: Compound average growth rate in sales, computed over a seven-year period (from 1982 through 1988).
- AVG NI/SALES: Profit margin, averaged over a six-year period (1983 through 1988).

For the retail, diversified financial, and diversified services industry groupings, sales and net income are defined in the typical manner and profit margin is calculated by dividing sales by net income.

TABLE 5
Rankings for Retail Companies (1982–1988)

Company Name	Sustainable Performance Index	Market Value 6-Yr. CAGR	Sales 6-Yr. Avg.	Sales 6-Yr. CAGR	Profit Margin 6-Yr. Avg.
LIMITED INC.	1	2	20	4	3
TOYS "Я" US INC.	2	15	22	7	4
WAL–MART STORES	3	5	6	3	11
NORDSTROM INC.	4	4	35	8	8
MAY DEPARTMENT STORES CO.	5	10	9	10	9
DILLARD DEPT. STORES CL A	6	1	31	9	10
MCDONALD'S CORP.	7	20	16	20	1
RITE AID CORP.	8	26	30	16	6
MARRIOTT CORP.	9	22	14	11	13
TANDY CORP.	10	30	19	22	2
MELVILLE CORP.	11	23	13	19	7
PRICE CO.	12	3	24	1	26
FOOD LION INC. CL A	13	9	25	5	22
AMES DEPT. STORES INC.	14	14	32	2	25
LOWE'S COS.	15	33	27	14	18
WALGREEN CO.	16	16	17	15	19

Company					
MERCANTILE STORES CO. INC.	17	19	28	29	5
DAYTON-HUDSON CORP.	18	32	7	18	17
CIRCLE K CORP.	19	13	26	6	29
SEARS, ROEBUCK & CO.	20	31	1	25	14
SERVICE MERCHANDISE CO.	21	29	23	12	32
US SHOE CORP.	22	24	29	21	23
PENNEY (J.C.) CO.	23	27	4	33	12
LONGS DRUG STORES INC.	24	25	33	24	21
WOOLWORTH (F.W.) CO.	25	8	11	30	16
AMERICAN STORES CO.– NEW	26	17	5	13	34
WICKES COS INC.	27	12	18	32	15
GREAT ATLANTIC & PAC. TEA CO.	28	7	10	17	31
GIANT FOOD INC.	29	6	21	27	24
K MART CORP.	30	21	2	26	27
ALBERTSON'S INC.	31	11	12	23	30
BROWN GROUP INC.	32	35	34	35	20
ZAYRE CORP.	33	18	15	31	28
KROGER CO.	34	34	3	28	35
WINN-DIXIE STORES INC.	35	28	8	34	33

TABLE 5 *(continued)*
Rankings for Diversified Services Companies (1982–1988)

Company Name	Sustainable Performance Index	Market Value 6-Yr. CAGR	Sales 6-Yr. Avg.	Sales 6-Yr. CAGR	Profit Margin 6-Yr. Avg.
CAPITAL CITIES/ABC INC.	1	12	18	4	5
WASTE MANAGEMENT INC.	2	16	28	7	3
DUN & BRADSTREET CORP.	3	17	16	14	2
DISNEY CO.	4	7	26	10	6
BROWNING-FERRIS INDS.	5	14	40	15	7
ITEL CORP.	6	1	69	1	23
MDC HOLDINGS INC.	7	70	73	2	25
COMDISCO INC.	8	18	58	17	11
AUTOMATIC DATA PROCESSING (ADP)	9	15	46	23	8
HUMANA INC.	10	48	21	24	12
RYLAND GROUP INC.	11	36	67	5	32
PHH	12	62	45	13	27
KELLY SERVICES INC.	13	8	55	12	29
AMERICAN MEDICAL INTL.	14	45	25	18	24
HILTON HOTELS CORP.	15	28	63	41	1
EMERSON RADIO	16	52	72	3	39
GRAINGER (W. W.) INC.	17	34	44	30	13
INTERPUBLIC GROUP OF COS.	18	13	61	26	19
UNITED STATIONERS INC.	19	11	70	9	37
RYDER SYSTEM INC.	20	32	10	22	26
PIONEER HI-BRED INTERNATIONAL	21	40	62	39	9
NIKE INC.	22	43	49	33	16
SERVICEMASTER	23	53	48	20	30

Company					
NATIONAL MEDICAL ENTERPRISES	24	55	17	29	22
GENUINE PARTS CO.	25	39	22	42	17
RYKOFF-SEXTON INC.	26	5	53	8	51
SYSCO CORP.	27	20	14	19	43
VIACOM INC.	28	6	65	6	56
BERGEN BRUNSWIG CORP.	29	41	19	11	53
HOLIDAY CORP.	30	69	33	50	14
HOSPITAL CORP. OF AMERICA	31	56	6	47	18
COMPUTER SCIENCES CORP.	32	21	54	32	33
CULBRO CORP.	33	30	59	25	40
CENTEX CORP.	34	66	39	35	31
BEVERLY ENTERPRISES	35	67	34	21	46
CBS INC.	36	26	7	65	4
FLEMING COMPANIES INC.	37	25	2	16	55
CAESARS WORLD	38	10	66	43	28
AVNET INC.	39	49	37	38	35
NASHUA CORP.	40	3	64	37	36
SUBARU OF AMERICA	41	63	36	36	38
SUPER VALU STORES INC.	42	38	1	28	49
GULF & WESTERN INC.	43	4	15	68	10
MCKESSON CORP.	44	37	3	34	47
WETTERAU INC.	45	22	8	27	54
GREYHOUND CORP.	46	44	20	61	21
NASH FINCH CO.	47	9	35	31	52
BLOUNT INC.	48	59	50	45	41
PS GROUP INC.	49	42	71	72	15
OGDEN CORP.	50	27	42	69	20
ALCO STANDARD CORP.	51	23	9	49	42
CBI INDUSTRIES INC.	52	64	43	51	44

TABLE 5 *(continued)*

Company Name	Sustainable Performance Index	Market Value 6-Yr. CAGR	Sales 6-Yr. Avg.	Sales 6-Yr. CAGR	Profit Margin 6-Yr. Avg.
TW SERVICES INC.	53	31	24	63	34
BALLY MFG CORP.	54	57	38	40	59
COMMERCIAL METALS CO.	55	19	52	54	48
CASTLE & COOKE INC.	56	2	32	48	58
TURNER CORP.	57	47	23	46	61
RAMADA INC.	58	24	68	58	50
DI GIORGIO CORP.	59	33	51	52	57
PERINI CORP.	60	50	60	56	60
MCA INC.	61	73	31	44	73
CHARTER CO.	62	60	27	73	45
WARNER COMMUNICATIONS INC.	63	29	13	53	66
MORRISON KNUDSEN CORP.	64	35	29	59	63
NATIONAL INTERGROUP INC.	65	51	12	55	68
ENSERCH CORP.	66	54	11	62	62
FISCHBACH CORP.	67	68	47	60	64
U S HOME CORP.	68	72	57	57	72
HALLIBURTON CO.	69	65	4	66	67
FLUOR CORP.	70	58	5	64	70
FARM HOUSE FOODS	71	71	56	70	65
PITTSTON CO.	72	46	41	67	71
TESORO PETROLEUM CORP.	73	61	30	71	69

TABLE 5 *(continued)*

Rankings for Diversified Financial Services Companies (1982–1988)

Company Name	Sustainable Performance Index	Market Value 6-Yr. CAGR	Sales 6-Yr. Avg.	Sales 6-Yr. CAGR	Profit Margin 6-Yr. Avg.
INTEGRATED RESOURCES	1	32	29	1	6
FLEET/NORSTAR FIN'L. GROUP	2	1	23	4	5
LOMAS & NETTLETON FIN'L.	3	19	30	2	8
SLMA	4	4	24	8	4
AON	5	9	21	10	3
GEICO	6	11	25	16	1
AMERICAN EXPRESS	7	14	4	7	15
LOEWS	8	3	8	12	10
CHUBB	9	2	16	9	13
GENERAL RE.	10	16	17	20	2
SAFECO	11	25	18	18	7
KAUFMAN & BROAD	12	5	26	5	20
USF & G	13	17	13	11	19
LANDMARK LAND	14	6	31	3	31

TABLE 5 (continued)
Rankings for Diversified Financial Services Companies (1982–1988)

Company Name	Sustainable Performance Index	Market Value 6-Yr. CAGR	Sales 6-Yr. Avg.	Sales 6-Yr. CAGR	Profit Margin 6-Yr. Avg.
CAPITAL HOLDING	15	22	19	26	9
KEMPER	16	7	14	19	17
CONTINENTAL	17	28	11	25	12
LINCOLN NATIONAL	18	13	10	15	23
PAINE WEBBER GROUP	19	12	20	13	26
SECURITY CAPITAL	20	33	32	6	33
MERRILL LYNCH	21	30	7	17	24
DCNY	22	10	33	30	11
TRANSAMERICA	23	21	9	21	21
ST. PAUL COS.	24	24	15	24	18
HOUSEHOLD INTERNATIONAL	25	15	12	32	14
ALEXANDER & ALEXANDER SRVCS	26	27	28	14	32
AETNA LIFE & CASUALTY	27	26	2	22	25
PRIMERICA	28	23	27	31	16
TRAVELERS CORP.	29	20	5	23	27
BENEFICIAL	30	18	22	29	22
CIGNA	31	29	3	27	28
FNMA	32	8	6	28	30
SALOMON	33	31	1	33	29

TABLE 5 *(continued)*
Rankings for Banks (1982–1988)

Banks	Sustainable Performance Index	Market Value 6-Yr. CAGR	Sales 6-Yr. Avg.	Sales 6-Yr. CAGR	Profit Margin 6-Yr. Avg.
PNC FINANCIAL CORP.	1	7	15	8	5
CORESTATES FINANCIAL CORP.	2	21	26	2	11
BANC ONE CORPORATION	3	28	22	5	9
FIRST UNION CORPORATION	4	6	16	4	12
OLD KENT FINANCIAL CORP.	5	20	64	14	3
TRUSTCORP, INC.	6	44	72	11	8
HIBERNIA CORPORATION	7	23	76	16	7
SOVRAN FINANCIAL CORPORATION	8	2	24	7	19
NATIONAL CITY CORPORATION	9	10	27	6	29
SOUTHTRUST CORPORATION	10	33	69	30	6
NCNB CORPORATION	11	14	18	19	22
UNITED JERSEY BANKS	12	5	47	15	26
KEYCORP	13	9	35	9	33
MARSHALL & ILSLEY CORP.	14	34	57	24	18
NBD BANCORP, INC.	15	24	25	29	15
REPUBLIC NEW YORK CORP.	16	38	37	44	1
SOCIETY CORPORATION	17	17	42	20	25

TABLE 5 (continued)
Rankings for Banks (1982–1988)

Banks	Sustainable Performance Index	Market Value 6-Yr. CAGR	Sales 6-Yr. Avg.	Sales 6-Yr. CAGR	Profit Margin 6-Yr. Avg.
SIGNET BANKING CORPORATION	18	13	39	13	34
BANK OF NEW ENGLAND CORP.	19	8	20	3	45
CITIZENS & SOUTHERN CORP.	20	22	23	17	31
BOATMEN'S BANCSHARES, INC.	21	4	52	1	47
MNC FINANCIAL, INC.	22	11	29	12	38
U.S. BANCORP	23	43	34	28	23
DOMINION BANKSHARES CORP.	24	30	53	21	30
J.P. MORGAN & CO. INC.	25	54	8	51	2
FIRST FLORIDA BANKS, INC.	26	60	70	50	4
BARNETT BANKS, INC.	27	19	17	18	37
BANCORP HAWAII, INC.	28	63	62	40	16
AMSOUTH BANCORPORATION	29	47	56	43	14
FIRST AMERICAN CORPORATION	30	25	61	22	35
FIRST OF AMERICA BANK CORP.	31	12	50	26	32
SOUTH CAROLINA NATIONAL CORP.	32	37	65	37	21
SHAWMUT CORPORATION	33	3	30	10	50

Company					
HUNTINGTON BANCSHARES INC.	34	26	46	27	39
STATE STREET BOSTON CORP.	35	35	38	32	36
AMERITRUST CORPORATION	36	49	43	48	20
BANKERS TRUST OF NEW YORK CORP.	37	48	9	52	17
INDIANA NATIONAL CORPORATION	38	18	67	42	28
CENTRAL BNCSHRS OF THE SOUTH	39	41	75	65	10
CRESTAR FINANCIAL CORP.	40	51	41	53	24
FIRST COMMERCE CORPORATION	41	68	73	23	55
BANK OF NEW YORK COMPANY	42	27	21	36	43
COMERICA INCORPORATED	43	45	36	38	42
UNITED MISSOURI BANCSHARES	44	56	74	68	13
SECURITY PACIFIC CORPORATION	45	32	4	25	58
BAYBANKS, INC.	46	39	44	39	44
FIRST WISCONSIN CORPORATION	47	40	45	33	57
WELLS FARGO & COMPANY	48	16	10	35	56
CITICORP	49	65	1	31	61
BANK OF BOSTON CORPORATION	50	53	12	41	51
FLORIDA NATIONAL BANKS OF FL.	51	70	48	45	48

TABLE 5 *(continued)*
Rankings for Banks (1982–1988)

Banks	Sustainable Performance Index	Market Value 6-Yr. CAGR	Sales 6-Yr. Avg.	Sales 6-Yr. CAGR	Profit Margin 6-Yr. Avg.
MANUFACTURERS NATIONAL CORP.	52	1	49	47	46
COMMERCE BANKSHARES, INC.	53	59	66	72	27
EQUITABLE BANCORPORATION	54	46	68	60	41
FIRST MARYLAND BANCORP	55	36	55	49	53
FIRST CHICAGO CORPORATION	56	50	11	34	69
CHEMICAL BANKING CORPORATION	57	62	7	46	59
FIRST TENNESSEE NATL. CORP.	58	57	54	59	49
RIGGS NATIONAL CORPORATION	59	52	71	71	40
SOUTHEAST BANKING CORP.	60	61	31	63	52
MICHIGAN NATIONAL CORP.	61	29	33	56	64
MERCANTILE BANCORP, INC.	62	64	51	67	54
NORTHERN TRUST CORPORATION	63	42	40	55	68
CHASE MANHATTAN CORPORATION	64	66	3	64	62

VALLEY NATIONAL CORPORATION	65	69	32	66	60
EQUIMARK CORPORATION	66	31	77	54	74
MANUFACTURERS HANOVER CORP.	67	74	5	62	67
MELLON BANK CORPORATION	68	76	13	57	73
FIRST PENNSYLVANIA CORP.	69	15	60	58	72
FIRST INTERSTATE BANCORP.	70	67	6	61	71
UNITED BANKS OF COLORADO	71	72	58	69	63
NORWEST CORPORATION	72	56	14	70	65
FIRST SECURITY CORPORATION	73	73	59	75	66
FIRST BANK SYSTEM, INC.	74	58	19	73	70
BANKAMERICA CORPORATION	75	71	2	74	75
FIRST CITY BANCORP OF TEXAS	76	75	28	77	76
TEXAS AMERICAN BANCSHARES	77	77	63	76	77

Sales = Net interest income + Total noninterest income

TABLE 5 *(continued)*
Rankings for Life Insurance Companies (1983–1987)

Insurance Group Name	Sustainable Performance Index	Insurance Revenue 4-Year AAGR	Operating Margin 6-Year Average
I.C.H. CORP.	1	3	4
MUTUAL OF AMERICA	2	11	1
LONDON INSURANCE (CANADA)	3	10	7
AMERICAN GENERAL	4	13	5
NEW ENGLAND MUTUAL	5	6	12
NORTH AMERICAN COMPANIES	6	16	3
NATIONWIDE	7	14	14
STATE FARM	8	22	8
I.D.S. FINANCIAL GROUP	9	8	24
NORTHWESTERN MUTUAL	10	20	19
PRINCIPAL FINANCIAL	11	17	22
LINCOLN NATIONAL	12	29	11
FRANKLIN LIFE	13	40	2
KEMPER	14	32	10
MUTUAL LIFE ASSURANCE (CANADA)	15	1	41
THE GUARDIAN	16	9	34
FIRST EXECUTIVE	17	7	37
NEW YORK LIFE	18	28	17
TRANSAMERICA	19	19	26
ALLSTATE	20	18	27
WESTERN AND SOUTHERN	21	41	6
CONTINENTAL CORP.	22	5	42
CIGNA GROUP	23	39	9

Company			
MANUFACTURERS LIFE (CANADA)	24	4	44
CROWN LIFE (CANADA)	25	2	48
PACIFIC MUTUAL LIFE	26	20	26
GENERAL AMERICAN LIFE	27	15	36
STATE MUTUAL COMPANIES	28	12	38
PROVIDENT LIFE AND ANNUITY	29	38	13
UNUM CORP.	30	30	21
PRUDENTIAL	31	27	25
MINNESOTA MUTUAL	32	23	30
MASSACHUSETTS MUTUAL	33	37	20
CONNECTICUT MUTUAL	34	34	23
HOME LIFE FINANCIAL	35	26	31
AETNA LIFE AND CASUALTY	36	43	15
MONY FINANCIAL	37	25	33
TRAVELERS	38	44	16
JOHN HANCOCK GROUP	39	42	18
MUTUAL BENEFIT LIFE	40	33	28
EQUITABLE	41	24	39
THE PHOENIX	42	31	36
METROPOLITAN INSURANCE	43	35	32
NATIONAL LIFE VERMONT	44	36	43
PENN MUTUAL	45	45	40
NORTH AMERICAN LIFE (CANADA)	46	46	45

Sales is replaced by insurance revenue, which consists of total premiums and investment income, minus claims, plus or minus changes in reserves. AAGR is used in place of CAGR because of data collection limitations.

Net income is replaced by operating net income, which consists of net gain from operations before dividends to policyholders and federal income taxes.

Profit margin is replaced by operating margin and is calculated by dividing total insurance income by operating net income.

TABLE 5 *(concluded)*
Rankings for Property and Casualty Companies (1983–1987)

Property and Casualty Companies	Sustainable Performance Index	Net Premiums 4-Yr. Avg.	Net Premiums 4-Yr. CAGR	Profit Margin 4-Yr. Avg.
GENERAL RE.	1	20	8	4
MOTORS INSURANCE	2	37	10	2
HARTFORD FIRE	3	21	12	1
EMPLOYERS RE.	4	36	7	6
AMERICAN INTERNATIONAL	5	4	4	10
PROGRESSIVE	6	44	2	13
CINCINNATI FINANCIAL	7	48	11	5
PMA INSURANCE	8	49	3	19
ERIE INSURANCE EXCHANGE	9	42	17	7
BERKSHIRE HATHAWAY	10	47	1	24
USAA	11	19	24	3
LINCOLN NATIONAL	12	22	5	26
GEICO	13	27	22	9
STATE FARM	14	1	27	8
AMERICAN FAMILY	15	34	20	17
CNA	16	11	6	32
AUTO-OWNERS	17	40	16	25
LIBERTY MUTUAL	18	9	13	30
ALLSTATE	19	2	29	15
GENERAL ACCIDENT	20	32	30	14
AUTOMOBILE CLUB OF MICH.	21	45	26	18
AETNA LIFE & CASUALTY	22	3	33	12
CALIFORNIA STATE AUTO ASSN.	23	39	18	29

Company				
PRUDENTIAL OF AMERICA (P & C Cos.)	24	38	31	11
NATIONWIDE	25	9	5	41
CHUBB	26	15	16	37
TRAVELERS	27	32	6	21
TRANSAMERICA	28	14	29	42
USF&G	29	19	12	38
SAFECO	30	35	26	22
ROYAL INSURANCE	31	23	18	36
OHIO CASUALTY	32	36	30	23
SOUTHERN FARM BUREAU	33	41	46	20
ASSOCIATED INSURANCE	34	48	33	16
FARMERS INSURANCE	35	31	7	34
CRUM AND FORSTER	36	21	14	45
AMERICAN GENERAL	37	28	25	39
ST. PAUL	38	37	15	31
INTERINS EXCH AUTO CLUB S CAL	39	43	41	28
SENTRY	40	39	38	33
KEMPER	41	47	35	27
ZURICH	42	25	43	49
CONTINENTAL INSURANCE	43	34	13	43
FIREMAN'S FUND	44	46	10	36
RELIANCE	45	45	24	40
CIGNA	46	40	8	47
HOME INSURANCE	47	44	17	44
AMERICAN FINANCIAL	48	42	23	48
COMMERCIAL UNION	49	49	28	46

Sales is replaced by net premiums.

TABLE 6
Data for Retail Companies (listed alphabetically)(1982–1988)

Company Name	Market Value 6-Yr. CAGR	Sales 6-Yr. Avg. (millions)	Sales 6-Yr. CAGR	Profit Margin 6-Yr. Avg.
ALBERTSON'S INC.	26.37%	$ 5,349.56	9.45%	1.90%
AMERICAN STORES CO.	18.33%	13,460.65	16.20%	1.13%
AMES DEPT STORES INC.	23.12%	1,663.80	42.02%	2.38%
BROWN GROUP INC.	1.67%	1,542.90	3.40%	2.79%
CIRCLE K CORP.	23.58%	2,129.18	25.49%	2.00%
DAYTON-HUDSON CORP.	5.24%	9,317.69	13.66%	2.97%
DILLARD DEPT STORES	46.20%	1,723.71	23.78%	4.12%
FOOD LION INC.	28.03%	2,280.58	26.14%	2.65%
GIANT FOOD INC.	30.07%	2,430.06	8.29%	2.44%
GREAT ATLANTIC & PAC. TEA CO.	29.97%	7,525.02	13.91%	1.58%
K MART CORP.	14.89%	23,383.75	8.51%	2.32%
KROGER CO.	3.81%	17,027.42	8.20%	0.79%
LIMITED INC.	39.49%	2,592.92	33.43%	6.57%
LONGS DRUG STORES INC.	11.36%	1,567.40	9.40%	2.75%
LOWE'S COS.	4.83%	2,072.40	15.98%	2.93%

MARRIOTT CORP.	14.55%	4,993.67	19.42%	3.65%
MAY DEPARTMENT STORES CO.	27.58%	7,795.11	21.39%	4.33%
MCDONALD'S CORP.	16.51%	4,096.54	12.56%	11.71%
MELVILLE CORP.	14.04%	5,182.42	12.97%	4.63%
MERCANTILE STORES CO. INC.	16.54%	1,943.71	7.99%	5.57%
NORDSTROM INC.	35.06%	1,491.54	24.91%	4.62%
PENNEY (J.C.) CO.	10.64%	14,107.34	5.00%	3.75%
PRICE CO.	37.90%	2,294.03	49.53%	2.33%
RITE AID CORP.	10.65%	1,890.73	14.18%	4.75%
SEARS, ROEBUCK & CO.	6.24%	43,066.36	8.97%	3.34%
SERVICE MERCHANDISE CO.	7.08%	2,330.12	17.17%	1.48%
TANDY CORP.	6.85%	3,055.92	10.96%	8.35%
TOYS "Я" US INC.	22.88%	2,429.86	25.14%	6.51%
U S SHOE CORP.	12.24%	1,943.21	10.98%	2.62%
WAL-MART STORES	34.96%	11,339.40	35.23%	4.01%
WALGREEN CO.	21.61%	3,515.47	15.66%	2.82%
WICKES COS INC.	24.27%	3,490.69	7.11%	3.19%
WINN-DIXIE STORES INC.	9.89%	8,022.04	4.89%	1.43%
WOOLWORTH CO.	29.46%	6,479.00	7.90%	2.99%
ZAYRE CORP.	18.20%	4,110.87	7.79%	2.24%

TABLE 6 *(continued)*
Data for Diversified Services Companies (listed alphabetically)(1982–1988)

Company Name	Market Value 6-Yr. CAGR	Sales 6-Yr. Avg. (millions)	Sales 6-Yr. CAGR	Profit Margin 6-Yr. Avg.
ALCO STANDARD CORP.	17.08%	$3,623.68	4.94%	1.95%
AMERICAN MEDICAL INTL.	5.86%	2,310.49	17.96%	4.25%
AUTOMATIC DATA PROCESSING	24.71%	1,134.90	15.01%	9.15%
AVNET INC.	3.73%	1,517.75	8.53%	3.15%
BALLY MFG. CORP.	−0.50%	1,429.57	7.54%	0.35%
BERGEN BRUNSWIG CORP.	8.32%	2,586.35	21.26%	0.91%
BEVERLY ENTERPRISES	−8.27%	1,723.35	16.60%	1.61%
BLOUNT INC.	−2.32%	1,072.71	6.25%	2.00%
BROWNING-FERRIS INDS.	24.83%	1,340.21	19.36%	9.96%
CAESARS WORLD	27.13%	689.60	6.87%	3.95%
CAPITAL CITIES/ABC INC.	26.69%	2,676.84	38.94%	11.57%
CASTLE & COOKE INC.	39.68%	1,771.43	5.18%	0.42%
CBI INDUSTRIES INC.	−5.25%	1,176.95	2.16%	1.82%
CBS INC.	14.66%	4,025.42	−6.10%	12.51%
CENTEX CORP.	−5.74%	1,386.43	9.51%	3.58%
CHARTER CO.	−3.27%	2,140.94	−29.69%	1.66%
COMDISCO INC.	23.41%	848.41	18.55%	7.91%
COMMERCIAL METALS CO.	22.96%	989.10	0.80%	1.27%
COMPUTER SCIENCES CORP.	19.59%	951.85	10.32%	3.35%
CULBRO CORP.	13.04%	834.71	14.06%	2.04%
DI GIORGIO CORP.	11.97%	1,040.91	2.14%	0.51%
DISNEY (WALT) COMPANY	28.85%	2,294.11	22.25%	10.38%
DUN & BRADSTREET CORP.	23.91%	2,903.11	19.55%	12.97%
EMERSON RADIO	3.50%	561.23	40.20%	2.11%
ENSERCH CORP.	2.25%	3,115.93	−5.26%	0.07%

Company				
FARM HOUSE FOODS	-17.02%	915.01	-11.48%	-0.75%
FISCHBACH CORP.	-8.28%	1,116.81	-5.08%	-0.74%
FLEMING COMPANIES INC.	16.82%	7,372.11	18.99%	0.71%
FLUOR CORP.	-1.07%	4,597.86	-5.78%	-2.36%
GENUINE PARTS CO.	9.02%	2,432.26	7.22%	5.45%
GRAINGER INC.	11.36%	1,174.48	11.40%	6.72%
GREYHOUND CORP.	7.24%	2,506.97	-5.10%	4.46%
GULF & WESTERN INC.	33.52%	2,984.21	-8.86%	8.75%
HALLIBURTON CO.	-5.48%	4,651.32	-6.63%	-1.24%
HILTON HOTELS CORP.	13.49%	738.46	7.31%	15.78%
HOLIDAY CORP.	-10.38%	1,763.29	3.48%	6.66%
HOSPITAL CORP. OF AMERICA	-0.29%	4,128.61	5.53%	5.20%
HUMANA INC.	3.84%	2,463.75	14.60%	7.33%
INTERPUBLIC GROUP OF COS.	24.90%	793.99	13.76%	5.12%
ITEL CORP.	91.48%	621.88	45.68%	4.38%
KELLY SERVICES INC.	27.68%	934.41	20.25%	3.88%
MCA INC.	-32.98%	1,792.64	6.82%	-5.19%
MCKESSON CORP.	10.06%	6,069.48	9.66%	1.35%
MDC HOLDINGS INC.	-14.03%	484.87	44.70%	4.19%
MORRISON KNUDSEN CORP.	10.77%	2,026.96	-3.40%	-0.32%
NASH FINCH CO.	27.26%	1,550.97	11.03%	0.92%
NASHUA CORP.	39.05%	722.98	8.76%	3.03%
NATIONAL INTERGROUP INC.	3.59%	3,088.18	-0.38%	-1.36%
NATIONAL MEDICAL ENTERPRISES	0.41%	2,840.63	11.92%	4.42%
NIKE INC.	7.33%	1,089.18	9.79%	5.47%
OGDEN CORP.	14.04%	1,272.80	-11.09%	4.89%
PERINI CORP.	3.66%	815.40	-2.38%	0.29%
PHH	-3.79%	1,136.81	20.17%	3.96%
PIONEER HI-BRED INTERNATIONAL	8.96%	773.67	7.80%	8.83%
PITTSTON CO.	4.12%	1,309.86	-6.83%	-2.41%
PS GROUP INC.	7.40%	580.69	-12.32%	5.96%
RAMADA INC.	17.00%	624.93	-2.71%	1.24%

233

TABLE 6 *(continued)*
Data for Diversified Services Companies (listed alphabetically)(1982–1988)

Company Name	Market Value 6-Yr. CAGR	Sales 6-Yr. Avg. (millions)	Sales 6-Yr. CAGR	Profit Margin 6-Yr. Avg.
RYDER SYSTEM INC.	12.27%	$3,530.29	15.89%	4.05%
RYKOFF-SEXTON INC.	30.26%	983.15	23.38%	1.17%
RYLAND GROUP INC.	10.48%	680.28	35.39%	3.40%
SERVICEMASTER	2.55%	1,105.28	17.07%	3.64%
SUBARU OF AMERICA	−5.24%	1,522.03	9.36%	2.44%
SUPER VALU STORES INC.	9.73%	8,184.86	12.07%	1.26%
SYSCO CORP.	20.87%	3,017.04	17.11%	1.91%
TESORO PETROLEUM CORP.	−3.35%	2,019.49	−12.12%	−1.98%
TURNER CORP.	4.04%	2,340.21	6.07%	0.28%
TW SERVICES INC.	12.27%	2,337.80	−5.78%	3.28%
U S HOME CORP.	−23.91%	911.08	−2.64%	−3.02%
UNITED STATIONERS INC.	26.98%	584.44	23.36%	2.59%
VIACOM INC.	29.63%	711.41	28.86%	0.62%
WARNER COMMUNICATIONS INC.	13.31%	3,023.61	0.88%	−1.03%
WASTE MANAGEMENT INC.	24.43%	2,053.53	24.30%	12.71%
WETTERAU INC.	19.58%	3,685.81	13.53%	0.88%

TABLE 6 *(continued)*

Data for Diversified Financial Companies (listed alphabetically)(1982–1988)

Company Name	Market Value 6-Yr. CAGR	Sales 6-Yr. Avg. (millions)	Sales 6-Yr. CAGR	Profit Margin 6-Yr. Avg.
AETNA LIFE & CASUALTY	6.57%	$19,221.19	9.41%	2.91%
ALEXANDER & ALEXANDER SRVCS	5.61%	902.92	14.36%	1.00%
AMERICAN EXPRESS	10.38%	15,470.00	18.96%	5.22%
AON	15.47%	1,814.93	17.39%	10.24%
BENEFICIAL	10.11%	1,530.78	−0.26%	4.08%
CAPITAL HOLDING	8.60%	2,196.45	8.04%	7.94%
CHUBB	25.22%	2,842.93	17.57%	6.32%
CIGNA	2.20%	15,899.80	7.20%	2.03%
CONTINENTAL	4.12%	5,226.76	8.97%	6.33%
DCNY	15.08%	210.60	−1.45%	7.20%
FLEET/NORSTAR FIN'L. GROUP	53.22%	1,481.11	33.22%	9.67%
FNMA	16.42%	9,822.46	6.80%	1.81%
GEICO	13.84%	1,300.53	13.55%	12.99%
GENERAL RE.	10.23%	2,497.27	10.56%	11.50%
HOUSEHOLD INTERNATIONAL	10.33%	4,739.17	−16.48%	5.84%
INTEGRATED RESOURCES	−9.02%	765.83	42.93%	9.06%
KAUFMAN & BROAD	20.16%	1,128.13	30.11%	4.16%

TABLE 6 *(continued)*
Data for Diversified Financial Companies (listed alphabetically)(1982–1988)

Company Name	Market Value 6-Yr. CAGR	Sales 6-Yr. Avg. (millions)	Sales 6-Yr. CAGR	Profit Margin 6-Yr. Avg.
KEMPER	16.99%	$ 3,044.29	11.73%	4.75%
LANDMARK LAND	17.32%	266.29	34.64%	1.32%
LINCOLN NATIONAL	11.51%	5,570.36	13.97%	3.76%
LOEWS	24.39%	7,307.20	14.84%	7.66%
LOMAS & NETTLETON FIN'L.	9.90%	528.68	39.02%	8.55%
MERRILL LYNCH	0.19%	8,295.40	13.15%	3.59%
PAINE WEBBER GROUP	12.56%	2,052.19	14.76%	2.69%
PRIMERICA	8.12%	1,122.32	– 1.97%	4.76%
SAFECO	7.40%	2,252.83	12.13%	8.60%
SALOMON	– 1.51%	23,433.67	– 21.72%	1.95%
SECURITY CAPITAL	– 26.86%	219.29	25.27%	– 7.33%
SLMA	24.28%	1,381.68	18.82%	9.89%
ST. PAUL COS.	7.49%	2,921.72	9.05%	4.61%
TRANSAMERICA	9.58%	6,133.29	10.51%	4.13%
TRAVELERS CORP.	9.75%	15,346.57	9.15%	2.35%
USF&G	10.20%	3,921.22	15.87%	4.29%

TABLE 6 *(continued)*

Data for Banks (listed alphabetically)(1982–1988)

Banks	Market Value 6-Yr. CAGR	Sales 6-Yr. Avg. (millions)	Sales 6-Yr. CAGR	Profit Margin 6-Yr. Avg.
AMERITRUST CORPORATION	14.80%	$ 333.26	13.16%	18.51%
AMSOUTH BANCORPORATION	25.97%	242.41	15.35%	19.69%
BANC ONE CORPORATION	29.23%	651.80	33.79%	21.87%
BANCORP HAWAII, INC.	21.21%	211.14	11.41%	19.21%
BANK OF BOSTON CORPORATION	19.09%	1,316.50	16.40%	11.87%
BANK OF NEW ENGLAND CORP.	54.18%	739.69	42.55%	14.74%
BANK OF NEW YORK COMPANY	18.58%	790.00	16.19%	15.36%
BANKAMERICA CORPORATION	−17.67%	5,598.94	5.94%	−3.37%
BANKERS TRUST NEW YORK CORP.	18.57%	1,755.97	17.11%	17.77%
BARNETT BANKS, INC.	35.33%	836.63	26.86%	16.11%
BAYBANKS, INC.	25.97%	323.29	14.42%	15.21%
BOATMEN'S BANCSHARES, INC.	43.24%	202.89	42.93%	16.35%
CENTERRE BANCORPORATION	10.25%	223.06	6.70%	10.58%
CENTRAL BNCSHRS. OF THE SOUTH	23.29%	144.61	11.09%	20.98%
CHASE MANHATTAN CORPORATION	2.26%	3,913.73	11.61%	7.08%
CHEMICAL BANKING CORPORATION	3.07%	2,321.89	14.21%	8.39%
CITICORP	7.33%	8,694.40	19.01%	8.22%
CITIZENS & SOUTHERN CORP.	34.45%	666.42	27.45%	17.23%
COMERICA INCORPORATED	20.46%	406.91	17.72%	14.77%
COMMERCE BANCSHARES, INC.	12.72%	210.58	8.78%	17.63%
CONTINENTAL ILLINOIS CORP.	−16.89%	1,047.01	−2.33%	−22.89%

TABLE 6 *(continued)*
Data for Banks (listed alphabetically)(1982–1988)

Banks	Market Value 6-Yr. CAGR	Sales 6-Yr. Avg. (millions)	Sales 6-Yr. CAGR	Profit Margin 6-Yr. Avg.
CORESTATES FINANCIAL CORP.	34.35%	$ 614.28	54.12%	21.08%
CRESTAR FINANCIAL CORP.	16.17%	351.13	15.59%	18.45%
DOMINION BANKSHARES CORP.	33.45%	242.86	21.85%	17.39%
EQUIMARK CORPORATION	30.28%	119.86	8.31%	−3.11%
EQUITABLE BANCORPORATION	24.05%	189.18	12.52%	15.44%
EUROPEAN-AMERICAN BANCORP.	4.81%	316.48	−1.95%	−12.25%
FIRST AMERICAN CORPORATION	35.31%	217.36	20.36%	18.32%
FIRST BANK SYSTEM	18.43%	865.37	9.52%	15.96%
FIRST CHICAGO CORPORATION	7.66%	1,596.66	15.74%	3.61%
FIRST CITY BANCORP OF TEXAS	−54.57%	621.40	−3.62%	−8.45%
FIRST COMMERCE CORPORATION	8.62%	142.91	20.99%	12.16%
FIRST FLORIDA BANKS, INC.	14.60%	186.85	15.79%	24.86%
FIRST INTERSTATE BANCORP	6.82%	2,529.60	11.67%	5.88%
FIRST KENTUCKY NATIONAL CORP.	24.87%	217.56	18.68%	18.19%
FIRST MARYLAND BANCORP	27.85%	245.58	15.81%	12.07%
FIRST OF AMERICA BANK CORP.	41.81%	265.08	18.91%	17.21%
FIRST PENNSYLVANIA CORP.	32.42%	236.32	12.04%	2.08%
FIRST REPUBLICBANK CORP.	−30.13%	749.93	10.40%	0.01%
FIRST SECURITY CORPORATION	0.20%	249.64	1.92%	7.83%
FIRST TENNESSEE NATL. CORP.	16.51%	261.85	14.10%	14.37%
FIRST UNION CORPORATION	52.26%	829.43	41.38%	20.86%
FIRST WISCONSIN	26.94%	316.42	13.58%	8.23%
FLORIDA NATIONAL BANKS OF FL.	5.08%	308.03	17.18%	15.70%
HIBERNIA CORPORATION	33.23%	125.77	26.52%	21.87%

HUNTINGTON BANCSHARES INC.	32.98%	305.27	20.73%	15.26%
INDIANA NATIONAL CORPORATION	35.87%	188.45	15.34%	17.50%
IRVING BANK CORPORATION	17.49%	800.05	11.53%	7.83%
J.P. MORGAN & CO., INC.	19.56%	2,235.19	13.49%	25.02%
KEYCORP	44.05%	369.18	33.60%	17.75%
MANUFACTURERS HANOVER CORP.	-6.23%	2,906.64	11.19%	3.64%
MANUFACTURERS NATIONAL CORP.	34.67%	282.72	12.92%	14.21%
MARSHALL & ILSLEY CORP.	27.64%	238.13	18.36%	18.79%
MCORP	-31.02%	698.08	10.19%	2.40%
MELLON BANK CORPORATION	0.36%	1,308.56	16.15%	1.75%
MERCANTILE BANCORP., INC.	10.26%	289.78	12.03%	12.91%
MICHIGAN NATIONAL CORP.	33.09%	426.80	14.29%	7.54%
MNC FINANCIAL, INC.	41.57%	486.71	29.34%	15.77%
NATIONAL CITY CORPORATION	37.49%	537.33	29.81%	17.50%
NBD BANCORP, INC.	33.33%	632.26	18.87%	19.35%
NCNB CORPORATION	26.36%	819.83	24.22%	18.29%
NORTHERN TRUST CORPORATION	19.88%	353.83	12.20%	4.54%
NORWEST CORPORATION	10.49%	1,146.14	9.17%	7.06%
OLD KENT FINANCIAL CORP.	30.55%	198.34	23.39%	25.30%
PNC FINANCIAL CORP.	51.08%	790.05	31.62%	23.03%
REPUBLIC NEW YORK CORP.	26.27%	365.03	14.77%	27.61%
RIGGS NATIONAL CORPORATION	13.28%	153.78	5.58%	15.87%
SECURITY PACIFIC CORPORATION	21.75%	2,795.79	20.38%	10.35%
SHAWMUT CORPORATION	58.03%	398.54	14.57%	12.71%
SIGNET BANKING CORPORATION	36.87%	337.85	27.67%	16.08%
SOCIETY CORPORATION	38.19%	339.20	24.28%	17.94%
SOUTH CAROLINA NATIONAL CORP.	24.58%	206.03	17.88%	18.56%
SOUTHEAST BANKING CORP.	10.63%	484.42	12.23%	13.13%

TABLE 6 *(continued)*
Data for Banks (listed alphabetically)(1982–1988)

Banks	Market Value 6-Yr. CAGR	Sales 6-Yr. Avg. (millions)	Sales 6-Yr. CAGR	Profit Margin 6-Yr. Avg.
SOUTHTRUST CORPORATION	33.41%	$ 184.56	16.57%	23.52%
SOVRAN FINANCIAL CORPORATION	63.20%	639.21	39.57%	18.35%
STATE STREET BOSTON CORP.	25.18%	362.65	16.88%	16.44%
TEXAS AMERICAN BANCSHARES	–32.05%	250.04	3.67%	–6.93%
TRUSTCORP. INC.	22.85%	131.28	33.54%	24.38%
U.S. BANCORP	20.92%	393.23	18.10%	18.70%
UNITED BANKS OF COLORADO	8.10%	252.10	11.62%	10.09%
UNITED JERSEY BANKS	55.19%	272.34	24.79%	17.47%
UNITED MISSOURI BANCSHARES	19.56%	144.30	8.96%	20.78%
VALLEY NATIONAL CORPORATION	12.44%	480.08	10.39%	9.90%
WELLS FARGO & COMPANY	29.02%	1,728.05	17.01%	10.60%

Sales = Net interest income + Total noninterest income.

TABLE 6 *(continued)*

Data for Life Insurance Companies (listed alphabetically) (1983–1987)

Insurance Group Name	Insurance Revenue 4-Year Avg.	Operating Margin 4-Year Avg.
AETNA LIFE AND CASUALTY	– 2%	4%
ALLSTATE	15%	2%
AMERICAN GENERAL	21%	12%
CIGNA GROUP	2%	9%
CONNECTICUT MUTUAL	6%	3%
CONTINENTAL CORP.	41%	– 2%
CROWN LIFE (CANADA)	92%	– 25%
EQUITABLE	10%	– 1%
FIRST EXECUTIVE	30%	0%
FRANKLIN LIFE	2%	17%
GENERAL AMERICAN LIFE	18%	1%
HOME LIFE FINANCIAL	10%	2%
I.C.H. CORP.	75%	13%
I.D.S. FINANCIAL GROUP	29%	3%
JOHN HANCOCK GROUP	1%	4%
KEMPER	7%	8%
LINCOLN NATIONAL	8%	7%
LONDON INSURANCE (CANADA)	26%	11%
MANUFACTURERS LIFE (CANADA)	57%	– 8%
MASSACHUSETTS MUTUAL	3%	4%
METROPOLITAN INSURANCE	5%	1%
MINNESOTA MUTUAL	11%	2%
MONY FINANCIAL	10%	1%
MUTUAL BENEFIT LIFE	6%	2%
MUTUAL LIFE ASSURANCE (CANADA)	97%	– 1%
MUTUAL OF AMERICA	24%	22%
NATIONAL LIFE VERMONT		– 3%
NATIONWIDE		5%

241

TABLE 6 *(continued)*
Data for Life Insurance Companies (listed alphabetically) (1983–1987)

Insurance Group Name	Insurance Revenue 4-Year AAGR	Operating Margin 4-Year Avg.
NEW YORK LIFE	8%	4%
NORTH AMERICAN LIFE (CANADA)	–47%	–19%
NORTH AMERICAN COMPANIES	18%	17%
NORTHWESTERN MUTUAL	12%	4%
PACIFIC MUTUAL LIFE	11%	2%
PENN MUTUAL	–7%	–1%
PRINCIPAL FINANCIAL	17%	3%
PROVIDENT LIFE AND ANNUITY	3%	5%
PRUDENTIAL	9%	2%
STATE FARM	11%	10%
STATE MUTUAL COMPANIES	22%	0%
THE GUARDIAN	28%	1%
THE PHOENIX	8%	1%
TRANSAMERICA	13%	2%
TRAVELERS	–3%	4%
UNUM CORP.	8%	4%
WESTERN AND SOUTHERN	2%	11%

Insurance revenue consists of total premiums and investment income, minus claims, plus or minus changes in reserves. AAGR is used in place of CAGR because of data collection limitations.

Operating net income consists of net gain from operations before dividends to policyholders and federal income taxes.

Operating margin is calculated by dividing operating net income by total insurance income.

TABLE 6 (continued)
Data for Property and Casualty Companies (listed alphabetically)(1983–1987)

Property and Casualty Companies	Net Premiums 4-Yr. Avg. (millions)	Net Premiums 4-Yr. CAGR	Profit Margin 4-Yr. Avg.	Net Income 4-Yr. AAGR
AETNA LIFE & CASUALTY	$5,158	12.89%	5.72%	57.48%
ALLSTATE	$8,410	14.14%	4.91%	0.24%
AMERICAN FAMILY	$1,015	16.28%	4.31%	283.12%
AMERICAN FINANCIAL	$1,473	7.87%	-7.14%	-1.16%
AMERICAN GENERAL	$1,261	14.25%	-1.20%	-93.20%
AMERICAN INTERNATIONAL	$4,681	34.07%	6.67%	27.34%
ASSOCIATED INSURANCE	$1,027	-1.01%	4.50%	-24.85%
AUTO-OWNERS	$702	20.67%	2.21%	61.67%
AUTOMOBILE CLUB OF MICH.	$585	14.85%	4.28%	162.65%
BERKSHIRE HATHAWAY	$515	48.85%	2.88%	116.96%
CALIFORNIA STATE AUTO ASSN.	$783	19.06%	1.71%	35.39%
CHUBB	$1,976	21.06%	-0.68%	-120.14%
CIGNA	$4,025	9.19%	-6.92%	-12.93%
CINCINNATI FINANCIAL	$498	23.42%	8.36%	22.61%
CNA	$2,909	30.91%	0.64%	14.72%
COMMERCIAL UNION	$1,129	-4.81%	-6.91%	75.05%
CONTINENTAL INSURANCE	$2,876	12.84%	-2.98%	22.57%
CRUM AND FORSTER	$2,553	16.21%	-4.65%	-473.01%
EMPLOYERS RE.	$986	28.82%	7.75%	26.91%
ERIE INSURANCE EXCHANGE	$615	19.83%	7.66%	55.82%
FARMERS INSURANCE	$4,146	13.80%	0.17%	248.29%
FIREMAN'S FUND	$3,048	4.54%	-0.61%	-156.15%
GEICO	$1,130	16.12%	7.18%	44.29%
GENERAL ACCIDENT	$1,034	13.82%	5.55%	333.13%
GENERAL RE.	$1,652	25.48%	9.08%	1,867.36%
HARTFORD FIRE	$1,559	22.60%	14.77%	59.89%

TABLE 6 (concluded)
Data for Property and Casualty Companies (listed alphabetically)(1983–1987)

Property and Casualty Companies	Net Premiums 4-Yr. Avg. (millions)	Net Premiums 4-Yr. CAGR	Profit Margin 4-Yr. Avg.
HOME INSURANCE	$1,768	6.60%	−4.47%
INTERINS EXCH. AUTO CLUBS OF CAL.	$677	7.47%	1.72%
KEMPER	$1,006	0.86%	1.95%
LIBERTY MUTUAL	$3,876	21.92%	1.39%
LINCOLN NATIONAL	$1,479	31.27%	2.20%
MOTORS INSURANCE	$894	23.44%	11.01%
NATIONWIDE	$4,487	23.62%	−1.91%
OHIO CASUALTY	$1,096	12.70%	3.01%
PMA INSURANCE	$448	40.10%	3.75%
PROGRESSIVE	$585	47.09%	5.67%
PRUDENTIAL OF AMERICA (P & C Cos.)	$1,034	11.13%	6.49%
RELIANCE	$1,354	6.45%	−1.37%
ROYAL INSURANCE	$1,723	15.95%	−0.15%
SAFECO	$1,170	12.71%	3.28%
SENTRY	$879	10.28%	0.52%
SOUTHERN FARM BUREAU	$576	8.51%	3.42%
ST. PAUL	$2,227	11.60%	1.37%
STATE FARM	$14,271	14.45%	7.47%
TRANSAMERICA	$1,110	21.85%	−2.21%
TRAVELERS	$4,292	13.00%	3.35%
USAA	$1,673	15.66%	9.86%
USF&G	$2,884	16.46%	−0.92%
ZURICH	$612	14.97%	−8.60%

Sales is replaced by net premiums.

TABLE 7
Retail Company List

The retail company list consists of 35 of the 50 retail organizations included in the *Fortune Service 500*, excluding the following 15 companies:

• Allied Stores	— Acquired by Campeau.
• Best	— Adler and Shakyn—January 1989.
• Carter Hawley Hale	— Restructuring and fiscal-year change.
• Cavenham (USA) Inc.	— Restructuring.
• Federated Department Stores	— Acquired by Campeau.
• Hills Department Stores	— Divested from SCOA Inds. December 1985.
• Lucky Stores Inc.	— Acquired by American Stores.
• Macy & Co.	— LBO.
• Montgomery Ward & Co.	— LBO (divested from Mobil June 1988).
• Payless Cashways	— Private—August 1988.
• Publix Super Markets	— Privately held.
• Revco D.S. Inc.	— LBO and bankruptcy.
• Safeway Stores Inc.	— LBO November 1986.
• Southland	— Private—1988.
• Stop & Shop Cos.	— LBO.

TABLE 7 *(continued)*
Diversified Services Company List

The diversified service company list consists of 73 out of 100 diversified financial organizations included in the *Fortune Service 500*, excluding the following 27 companies:

• Alco Health Services Corp.	— Incorporated in June 1985.
• Allegheny Beverage	— Owned by Pepsi-Cola Co.
• American Hardware Supply Co.	— Privately held (Service Star).
• AMFAC	— Private—1988.
• ARA Holdings	— Privately held.
• Associated Milk Producers	— Cooperative.
• Atkinson (G.F.) Co.	— Privately held prior to 1985.
• Berkshire Hathaway	— Listed as a property and casualty company.
• Bindley Western Inds.	— Privately held in 1982.
• Charter Medical	— Cooperative.
• Countrymark	— Private—August 1988.
• Dairymen	— Cooperative.
• Electronic Data Systems	— Privately held.
• Geico	— Delisted from Exchange in December 1987.
• Henley Group Inc.	— Spun off from Allied Signal in June 1986.
• Hertz Corp.	— Privately held by RCA (1982–85) and UAL (1985–87).
• Indiana Farm Bureau	— Cooperative.
• IU international	— Privately held; delisted from Exchange in May 1988.
• Kay Corp.	— Changed to Balfour Maclaine Corp. in 1988.
• Lorimar	— Acquired by Warner Communications in 1988.
• Maxicare Health Plans Inc.	— Went public in 1983.
• Pulte Home Corporation	— Became subsidiary of PHM Corp. in December 1987.
• Reebok International Ltd.	— Went public in 1985.
• Roundy's Inc.	— Privately held.
• Sunkist Growers	— Cooperative.
• Super Food Services Inc.	— Privately held.
• Telex	— Privately held.

TABLE 7 *(continued)*
Diversified Financial Services Company List

The diversified financial company list consists of 33 out of 50 diversified financial organizations included in the *Fortune Service 500*, excluding the following 17 companies:

- American Financial Corp.   — Private company.
- American International Grp.   — Listed as a property and casualty company.

- Argonaut Group   — IPO October 1986, spun off by Teledyne.

- Barclays American Corp.   — Private company.
- Bear Stearns Cos.   — IPO October 1985.
- Commercial Credit Corp.   — Merged with Primerica Corp. December 1988.

- Farmers Group, Inc.   — Listed as a property and casualty company.

- Fireman's Fund   — IPO October 1985—spun off from Am. Ex.

- First Boston   — Private—December 1988.
- Hanover Insurance Cos.   — 51% owned by State Mutual Ins. Co.
- Home Group   — IPO August 1985.
- Morgan Stanley Group   — IPO March 1986.
- Ohio Casualty   — Listed as a property and casualty company.

- Old Republic   — Data were not available.
- Reliance Group Holdings   — IPO September 1986.
- Southmark   — Filed Chapter 11.
- U.S. Leasing   — Acquired by Ford Motor Co. December 1987.

TABLE 7 *(continued)*
Bank List

The bank list consists of 77 out of 100 commercial banking companies included in the *Fortune Service 500,* excluding the following 23 companies:

• California First Bank	— Subsidiary of Bank of Tokyo.
• Centerre	— Data were not available
• Continental	— Data were not available
• Banco Popular de Puerto Rico	— Subsidiary of Banco Popular P.R.
• Bank of Tokyo Trust	— Subsidiary of Bank of Tokyo.
• European-American Corp.	— Data were not available
• First American Bancshares	— Privately held.
• First Fidelity Bancorp.	— New company as a result of a February 1988 merger.
• First Kentucky	— Data were not available
• First Republic Bank	— Data were not available
• First Wachovia Corp.	— New company as a result of a December 1985 merger.
• Harris Bankcorp.	— Subsidiary of Bank of Montreal.
• Irving Bank	— Data were not available
• MCorp.	— Data were not available
• Marine Corp.	— Subsidiary of Bank One Corp., Columbus, Ohio.
• Marine Midland Banks	— Acquired as a subsidiary of Hong Kong Bank, December 1985.
• Meridian Bancorp., Inc.	— New company as a result of a 1982 merger.
• Midlantic Banks	— Administrative entity.
• National Westminster Bank USA	— Subsidiary of National Westminster PLC.
• Premier Bancorp.	— New company as a result of a December 1988 merger.
• Ranier Bancorp.	— Subsidiary of Security Pacific.
• Suntrust Banks, Inc.	— Merged with Trust Co. of Georgia in 1984.
• Union Bancorp.	— Subsidiary of First Union Bancorp.

Life Insurance Company List

The life insurance company list consists of all life insurance companies in the *Fortune Service 500.*

TABLE 7 *(concluded)*
Property and Casualty Company List

The property and casualty company list consists of 49 of the top 50 property and casualty companies based on a ranking of admitted assets, excluding the following company:

• America Group   — Lead company is Hanover Insurance Co. (see diversified financial company list).

For banks, sales are defined by adding net interest income to total noninterest income. Net income and profit margin are defined as they are in the other industry groupings.

For property and casualty companies, sales are replaced by net premiums. Net income and profit margin are defined as they are in the other industry groups. Property and casualty data are current only through 1987.

For life insurance companies, sales are replaced by insurance revenues, which consist of total premiums and investment income minus claims, plus or minus changes in reserves. Also, due to limitations in data collection, we use an average annual growth rate in place of a compound annual growth rate for this variable. Net income is replaced by operating net income, which consists of net gain from operations before dividends to policyholders and federal income taxes. Profit margin, which is replaced by operating margin, is calculated by dividing operating net income by total insurance income. Life insurance data are current only through 1987.

The SPI is developed by taking the sum of the profit margin and sales CAGR-ranked variables (shown in Table 5) for each of the companies in our data base and then reranking the new variable; a low rank indicates a good performer and a high rank indicates a relatively poor performer. The variables comprising the SPI are given equal weight for simplicity and because the coefficients of each of the independent variables were approximately equal. Furthermore, the rankings did not change appreciably when the coefficients of the regression equations were used as weights to create the Index. The SPI is presented in Table 5 for each of the Fortune Service 500 group of companies as well as the two insurance company groupings.

Industry Impacts

In the course of our analysis, we tested an SPI based on AAGR NI, CAGR SALES, and AVG NI/SALES because AAGR NI, though volatile, was strongly correlated with market value. Interestingly, there was little movement within the top and bottom 10 companies in the Index except for the retail sector. Due to the volatility of net income which resulted in unreliable growth rates and averages, AAGR NI, average annual growth rate in net income was not included in the SPI. Although we believe the two-variable formulation is superior to this three-variable formulation, the change in SPI components made little difference. Table 8 reflects the change that restructuring the SPI had on the SPI final index. The retail industry (see Table 8) was the only industry sector that sustained a significant shift as a result of the change in index components. For example, when comparing the top three performers of the old and new indexes, the top three on the old index are not represented in the new index. Likewise, four bottom performers represented in the old index are not represented in the new index.

Other industry differences are apparent in the data. Analysis of each industry grouping showed the following industry variations:

- The average annual growth rate in net income is the most significant independent variable in explaining market value in the retail industry.
- The compound annual-growth rate in sales is the most significant variable in explaining market value in the diversified services sector.
- Profit margin is the most significant variable in explaining market value in the diversified financial sector (excluding P & C insurance companies); however, it is a weak explanatory variable.
- The average annual growth rate in net income is the most significant independent variable in explaining market value in the P & C insurance sector.

TABLE 8
Comparison of Alternative Indexes

	Change in Top Performers	Change in Bottom Performers
Retail	3	4
Diversified Services	1	1
Diversified Financial	2	1
Banks	1	1

- The compound annual growth rate in sales (net interest earnings and fee income) is the strongest explainer of market value in the banking sector. However, the average annual growth rate in net income and profit margin are also strong explanatory variables.

Though industry variation exists, construction is based on the aggregate industry analysis because the number of companies in industry-specific samples was too small for reliability.

Size as a Factor in the SPI

In general, size is not a definitive indicator of company performance—at least for the companies in our data base. The importance of size as an indicator of company performance is controversial because there is a growing feeling that small companies outperform large companies. In other words, the larger the company, the worse its performance and the lower its market value. The March 27, 1989 issue of *Business Week* is evidence that the controversy rages as indicated by the cover story entitled "Is Your Company Too Big?" Our analysis shows that for companies in our data base—all preselected because they are largest in their industry grouping—a strong size bias does not exist.

A size ranking was developed by using the company in the data base with the largest sales as the base—with all other companies evaluated as a percentage of the base. For example, a ranking of "1" indicates that it is the company having the highest sales in the industry group (see Tables 5 and 6). In general, there is no strong correlation between the size of a company and market value. When taken separately, none of the industries showed a strong correlation between company size and market value. The diversified services industry showed a marginally stronger correlation than the other industries tested with a correlation factor of minus .1888. The interpretation of a negative correlation is that the larger a company, the lower its market value.

We also tested the correlation between size and the SPI to determine whether the SPI was biased by company size. Bias in the index can mechanically be introduced because, mathematically, it is easier to grow from a small base than a large base. Therefore, a performance indicator such as the compound annual-growth rate in sales would reward small companies in the index.

TABLE 9
Performance versus Size of Company Correlations

Industry Group	Size versus Market Value	Size versus the SPI
Retail	(.0860)	(.2360)
Diversified Services	(.1888)	(.3047)
Diversified Financial*	(.0864)	(.4148)
Banks	(.2862)	(.2675)
Life Insurance Companies	N/A	N/A

The results show that there is no strong correlation between company size and the SPI. The relatively low correlation between size and the SPI, in most industry sectors, is explained by the fact that the sample is based on the Fortune Service 500, which by definition, is comprised of large companies. In addition, profit margin, one of the three independent variables comprising the SPI, is a ratio and does not have a size bias. Table 9 shows the correlations for both market value and the SPI versus company size.

Top and Bottom Performers

Based on our analysis of companies in *The Fortune Service 500,* we identified a number of company-performance variables that correlate with market value and are reasonable differentiators of good versus poor performance by companies. However, past performance is not necessarily an indicator of future performance. It is not an indicator of a company's expected revenues or of profit potential from either existing or anticipated investments. For that reason, our list of top and bottom performers uses both the market value and the SPI to select top and bottom performers. Specifically, a top performer is any company that achieved a SPI ranking *and* a market-value ranking within the top quartile of its industry group; a bottom performer is a company that was in the bottom quartile based on the two rankings. Table 10 identifies top performers based on this criteria; Table 11 presents bottom performers.

Neither of these lists is exhaustive. These lists represent the subset of firms that, based on the criteria we have described, are repeated top or bottom performers. The life and property and casualty companies are not shown in Tables 11 and 12 because most of them are mutual companies, and as such, do not have market values.

TABLE 10
Top Performers

Company	Industry
Aon	Diversified Financial
Fleet/Norstar Financial Group	Diversified Financial
Loews	Diversified Financial
SLMA	Diversified Financial
Dillard Dept. Stores	Retail
Limited, Inc.	Retail
Nordstrom Inc.	Retail
Wal-Mart stores	Retail
Automatic Data Processing	Diversified Services
Browning-Ferris Ind.	Diversified Services
Capital Cities/ABC	Diversified Services
Comdisco Inc.	Diversified Services
Disney Company	Diversified Services
Dun & Bradstreet	Diversified Services
Interpublic Group of Cos.	Diversified Services
ITEL Corp.	Diversified Services
Kelly Services Inc.	Diversified Services
Waste Management	Diversified Services
Bank of New England Corp.	Bank
First Union Corp.	Bank
Keycorp	Bank
National City Corporation	Bank
NCNB Corporation	Bank
PNC Financial	Bank
Signet Banking Corp.	Bank
Society Corporation	Bank
Sovran Financial Corporation	Bank
United Jersey Banks	Bank

TABLE 11
Bottom Performers

Company	Industry
Aetna Life & Casualty	Diversified Financial
Alexander & Alexander	Diversified Financial
CIGNA	Diversified Financial
Salomon	Diversified Financial
Brown Group.	Retail
Kroger Co.	Retail
Winn-Dixie Stores Inc.	Retail
Charter Co.	Diversified Services
Farm House Foods	Diversified Services
Fischbach Corp.	Diversified Services
Fluor Corp.	Diversified Services
Halliburton Co.	Diversified Services
MCA Inc.	Diversified Services
Tesoro Petroleum Corp.	Diversified Services
U.S. Home Corp.	Diversified Services
Bankamerica Corporation	Bank
Chase Manhattan Corporation	Bank
First City Bancorp of Texas	Bank
First Interstate Bancorp	Bank
First Security Corporation	Bank
Manufacturers Hanover Corp.	Bank
Mellon Bank Corporation	Bank
Mercantile Bancorp., Inc.	Bank
Southeast Banking Corp.	Bank
Texas American Bancshares	Bank
United Banks of Colorado	Bank
Valley National Corporation	Bank

CONCLUSIONS

Having identified top and bottom performers in the service industry, the natural next step is to identify the causal factors that distinguish the top from bottom performers. We attempted to define the characteristics that underlie sustained economic and financial performance in Chapter 8. To briefly restate the conclusions, we inferred the following as characteristics of successful service institutions, while at the same time, suggested that the opposite characteristics *might* be present in less successful organizations:

- A focus on served market—"not all things to all people."
- Relatively lean, cost-effective organizational structures—"a few good people, yielding high margins."
- Consistency—the long view versus an undue focus on quarterly earnings.
- A high ratio of variable to fixed costs.
- Innovative use of technology.
- Networking, that is, sourcing of services/"products."
- Leadership versus management.
- High barriers to entry: human capital and relationships.

Characteristics listed above and described in more detail in Chapter 8 would be the starting point for an analysis of the top and bottom performers identified. For example, a comparison of organizational productivity, cost structures, and technological innovation might reveal significant differences between the top and bottom performers, thereby identifying actions that can be taken to influence shareowners value. Even in those instances in which business cycles appear to explain relatively poor performance (i.e., the weakness in the Texas market because of the fall in oil prices and problematic international loan portfolios for banks), we can still learn from the firms that, despite industry difficulties, manage to repeatedly remain on top.

INDEX